Stable Help

What My Horses Helped Me Learn About God

Connie Van Huis

Copyright © 2017 Connie Van Huis

All rights reserved. No part of this book may be used or reproduced by any means, graphic, electronic, or mechanical, including photocopying, taping or by any information storage retrieval system without the written permission of the author except in the case of brief quotations embodied in critical articles and reviews.

Scripture quotations are from the ESV Bible® (The Holy Bible, English Standard Version®), copyright © 2001 by Crossway, a publishing ministry of Good News Publishers. Used by permission. All rights reserved.

Pictured on the cover: CJ and Skipper

ISBN: 1539637875
ISBN-13: 978-1539637875

I am grateful to God that he gave us his Word, the Bible, so we don't have to wonder what he is like or how we are supposed to live. I am also grateful that he takes the time to train me in such a patient and kind way, knowing exactly how I learn the best so I can be useful to him.

Thanks also to my family, who endured my divided attention as I struggled to understand my horses and learned to be a trainer. Their help made having horses possible and the reason I have so many stories.

CONTENTS

1.	The Payment	1
2.	The Purpose	7
3.	Not The Purpose	11
4.	Lead	16
5.	Copy That	21
6.	Fenced In	27
7.	Not a Suggestion	31
8.	Rest	36
9.	Owning It	41
10.	Contentment	48
11.	Useless	53
12.	The One Thing	58
13.	The Curse	63
14.	Bad Credit	67
15.	Lagging	71
16.	Free	75
17.	Touch It	80
18.	Sneaker	84
19.	Label Maker	89
20.	Runaway	94
21.	Transplanted	99
22.	Crisis Reveals	105
23.	Realizing It	110
24.	Come	114
25.	No Further	118
26.	Walking With	123
27.	Love It, Hate It	128
28.	Inconsistent	136
29.	Connect	140
30.	New	146
31.	Making the Trail	151
	About the Author	156

FOREWORD

Thirty-one stories await you in this book. A month's worth if you read one every day. The stories you're about to read all really happened to my horses and me. I'll be telling you what I learned, and maybe you'll see a different lesson from the same story. God has a special purpose in mind for each of us when he works with us, just like we have when we work with a horse. We want the best for them. We know their potential. We know the end of it. They just need to trust and obey.

Connie Van Huis

A verse to hang your hat on: "Make me to know your ways, O LORD; teach me your paths. Lead me in your truth and teach me, for you are the God of my salvation; for you I wait all the day long." – Psalm 25:4-5

Read about it in Psalm 103:8-22

[8] The LORD is merciful and gracious, slow to anger and abounding in steadfast love. [9] He will not always chide, nor will he keep his anger forever. [10] He does not deal with us according to our sins, nor repay us according to our iniquities. [11] For as high as the heavens are above the earth, so great is his steadfast love toward those who fear him; [12] as far as the east is from the west, so far does he remove our transgressions from us. [13] As a father shows compassion to his children, so the LORD shows compassion to those who fear him. [14] For he knows our frame; he remembers that we are dust. [15] As for man, his days are like grass; he flourishes like a flower of the field; [16] for the wind passes over it, and it is gone, and its place knows it no more. [17] But the steadfast love of the LORD is from everlasting to everlasting on those who fear him, and his righteousness to children's children, [18] to those who keep his covenant and remember to do his commandments. [19] The LORD has established his throne in the heavens, and his kingdom rules over all. [20] Bless the LORD, O you his angels, you mighty ones who do his word, obeying the voice of his word! [21] Bless the LORD, all his hosts, his ministers, who do his will! [22] Bless the LORD, all his works, in all places of his dominion. Bless the LORD, O my soul!

1
THE PAYMENT

So much excitement. We all got up early. I was first, because it works best when the mom gets everyone else up in the right order. I brought the boys to Grandma's. My husband, Wayne, fired up the dually and left to go get my brother's horse trailer because we didn't have one of our own, yet. Janelle rode with Wayne, feeling excited and anxious and happy and nervous all at the same time.

Today was buy-Janelle's-first-horse day.

The big horse auction we were headed to was about an hour and a half away. Riding horses didn't start going through the ring until 1:00 p.m., but we wanted to get there plenty early so we could look around and meet some prospects.

Now, buying a horse at an auction is a tricky business. Of course, buying any horse, from anywhere, is tricky business. Buying at an auction carries a good deal of risk, and one must know some things. I knew a couple of people who regularly bought horses at auctions and sold them again. We called them horse traders. From talking to them, I felt prepared as we sped toward the highway, trailer in tow, a giddy daughter on one side of me and a somewhat wary husband on the other.

When we arrived, there were about 100 horses in the huge auction barn, and more coming in pretty steadily. Quite a few of them were draft horses, the lot of which were being sold starting at 10 a.m. We petted a few of their long faces as we went by on the way to the area they designated for the riding horses. We passed a pen that held four Shetland ponies, then one that contained two, enormous-eared donkeys. One of them started to bray, and, probably because it was in a big barn, it was one of the loudest noises I've ever heard. We burst out laughing. It was a very humorous sound!

Unsure what we were looking for, just certain we would know the horse when we saw it, we paused at each pen we came to, evaluating the horse or horses within. In a very large pen toward the middle, there were five horses tied to the fence rails. The one closest to the aisle was a dun mare. Now, I know you're not supposed to get all wrapped up in a horse's color and you're supposed to look past it, but we were pretty much hooked right then. She was a dark golden color with black on her legs that went up past her knees and ended in tiger stripes. She stood about 13.2 hands (at four inches per hand, that's 54 inches at the wither). She was a very nice size for Janelle to start off with. We went inside the pen to talk to the owner, who was brushing the horse next to the dun mare.

She told us she had brought the five horses up from Tennessee for the sale. That was a pretty long haul, and I thought right away the prices she would want for her horses were probably going to make it hard for us to afford the mare. We asked her how old the dun was, and if she was a good riding horse. She told us the mare's name was Angel, and she was twelve years old. She had been riding with

THE PAYMENT

the saddle and bareback and had started working the pony over cross poles. Janelle was taking lessons with a trainer who had hunter/jumpers and had even competed in a jumping event using the trainer's lesson horse, so that sounded good to us. The lady also introduced us to the horse she was brushing and added that we could feel free to go up and meet all of her horses as they were all gentle and good broke riding horses. Janelle was only interested in petting Angel, especially since she was on the small side. The other four ranged from big to even bigger. Besides, Janelle was already hooked on the little mare. Even though we looked at a lot of other horses before the bidding started at 1:00, she kept going back to Angel to talk to her and stroke her soft, golden neck.

We filed into the seating area around the ring at about 12:30. The ring was quiet, but the seats held a good number of people waiting for the riding horses to start coming in. Although a bunch of horses would be bid on before Angel, we were ready to sit for a while and watch how it all worked. Janelle was worried the money she had brought wouldn't be enough. She had been saving up for about three years. Birthday money, Christmas money, odd jobs, and a few other things had created her little horse fund. She really, really wanted Angel and hadn't found another horse as a backup plan if Angel's price went too high for her savings. All that added up to one little bundle of nerves. The half-hour interim flew by and soon horses were entering the ring, being bid on, and exiting, all in kind of a smooth parade serenaded by an unintelligible chant.

Anxious waiting finally came to an end. The lady from Tennessee, mounted on Angel, rode into the ring. Janelle and I were leaving the bidding to Wayne, who was much more savvy about auctions and could actually understand what the auctioneer

THE PAYMENT

was saying. We girls listened to the sing-song chanting peppered with numbers, agonizingly keeping our eyes glued to the pair in the ring. Wayne surreptitiously nodded. The sing-song got more intense. Wayne nodded again. At a kind of subconscious level, I noticed there was movement in the crowd. People were chatting, leaving, coming in...because what was going on in our little corner of the world didn't matter to them. Then, in what seemed like a moment, or an eternity, it was over. The lady rode out of the ring.

"Did we get her?" Janelle and I asked at the same time.

"Yes, we did," Wayne nodded. "Let's go see your new horse and get our paperwork."

Janelle and I squealed like a couple of schoolgirls and tried not to run out of the room, though we did trot down the stairs at a pretty good pace. She hugged Angel and beamed at the lady from Tennessee, who had no trouble guessing who had just bought the mare.

We left the pen where Angel was tied and got in line at the "buyers" window. When it was our turn to pay, Janelle pulled out her stash. It was smiles all around the room as the teller at the window began counting out dozens of fives and ones, then began separating the coins into piles for counting. Janelle watched the money she had so painstakingly saved and worked for become neatly stacked next to the cash register. There was enough to cover the purchase price. Angel was officially hers, and Janelle had a pink slip to prove it.

Now, if someone said to you, "Angel should pay her purchase price", you would look at them like they were crazy. The dun mare didn't have the currency. It wouldn't have mattered if Angel could have counter-cantered a thirty-foot circle, or jumped a six-foot fence, or run a mile in 1.32 flat. Nothing

THE PAYMENT

she could do would have helped her become ours and come home with us. She didn't have what it took to make the payment.

We are so funny. We get all wound up about making sure we're good enough to get into heaven. Or we can be pretty sure we're in as long as we haven't done too much bad. But what we do, or don't do, is not the payment required. When God told Adam not to eat the fruit of the Tree of Knowledge of Good and Evil, he said if Adam did, he would die (Genesis 2:16,17). Now, I know he didn't drop dead when he ate it, but we don't think about death right when we think that way. Sin results in death, and death means "separation". Separation from God first, this mortal life later, and from God forever if something isn't done about it. Death is the payment for sin. God never said to do a bunch of good things to make up for doing bad things. And the goal isn't getting into heaven; the goal is being right with God, to not be separated anymore. It is a *position*, not a *location*. The location comes later, from the position. Kind of like you don't get the office with the window until you have a title after your name.

Here's something to consider: When Christ so painstakingly paid the price for our redemption, he paid it all, all by himself. He did it by dying in our place, for our sin. Jesus paid our ransom with his own blood. He did it all; nothing we do can make us right with God. Because of the death of Christ, the debt is stamped "paid", and a person becomes a child of God. That's the position. That's where the new life, the new adventure, begins.

A verse to hang your hat on: "...knowing that you were ransomed from the futile ways inherited from your forefathers, not with perishable things such as silver or gold, but with the precious blood of Christ, like that of a lamb without blemish or spot." –

THE PAYMENT

1 Peter 1:18-19

Read about it in Ephesians 2:1-10.

¹ And you were dead in the trespasses and sins ² in which you once walked, following the course of this world, following the prince of the power of the air, the spirit that is now at work in the sons of disobedience-- ³ among whom we all once lived in the passions of our flesh, carrying out the desires of the body and the mind, and were by nature children of wrath, like the rest of mankind. ⁴ But God, being rich in mercy, because of the great love with which he loved us, ⁵ even when we were dead in our trespasses, made us alive together with Christ--by grace you have been saved-- ⁶ and raised us up with him and seated us with him in the heavenly places in Christ Jesus, ⁷ so that in the coming ages he might show the immeasurable riches of his grace in kindness toward us in Christ Jesus. ⁸ For by grace you have been saved through faith. And this is not your own doing; it is the gift of God, ⁹ not a result of works, so that no one may boast. ¹⁰ For we are his workmanship, created in Christ Jesus for good works, which God prepared beforehand, that we should walk in them.

2
THE PURPOSE

One day a friend called and asked if we were interested in an older gelding her friend was looking to re-home. She said he was a horse anyone could ride, plus he was gaited. I had never ridden a gaited horse, but my friend said they were smooth and more fun to ride than a trotting horse. She was sure he was worth checking out.

We drove the hour and a half to look at this gelding, trailer in tow. Turns out he was twenty-six years old, and his owner was looking for a place to retire him. In his day, he had been a three-time World Champion Paso Fino. He was a dark buckskin with little, cute, fuzzy ears. His finely arched neck was wide and thick, and his shoulders were massive. His back was swayed some with age, but not too bad. His attitude was gentle and wise. He lowered his head slowly to delicately touch Janelle's hair. We liked him immediately. We knew someone who had a quarter horse nearing 30, so his age didn't scare us. We were looking for a friend, and we had found one.

We also found out his people called him Raisin, which we didn't care for. It seemed like a three-time World Champion should have a more respectful barn name. He had a really long, cool registered name on his papers, which did not in any way lend itself to a nickname. On the way home, with him safely ensconced in our trailer, we decided on Cheyenne. It would sound a little like Raisin at the end when we said it so he could be comfortable with it. Then again, Cheyenne sounds like "ann" at the end, and Raisin ends with "in", but we had faith in his ability to overlook the English. Funny, all that brainstorming to come up with a name, and we ended up calling him The Old Guy. We just said it with respect.

    We turned him out in the piece of hayfield we had fenced in for the winter, and he gladly dropped his nose into the deep grass. Angel stood on tiptoe as we led him in, but he ignored her. For a few minutes he ate voraciously. His euphoria was rudely interrupted by a dash of hoofbeats as Angel thundered up, whipped around, and barrel-kicked him. Cheyenne's head flew up in anger. He squealed, turned his haunches in her direction, and bunny-hopped backward toward her, squealing with every hop. Angel ran. We applauded. What a cool old guy. He was in charge not only of a mare, but a pony mare at that!

    So began the love affair between The Old Guy and Janelle. His physique grew stronger with the grazing and her simple riding. Mostly she rode bareback. He was smooth indeed. She wasn't afraid to run him back toward the barn from the far reaches of the hayfield, because they were just running, not running in. He leaped the little drainage swale along the trees without missing a step. He loved to see her coming out to ride. He lowered his head for the bridle. He would buck if someone else got on him. Well, buck as well as a Paso Fino can (which is not impressive in my experience) a couple of times to express his displeasure, then he would move on. It made Janelle beam.

THE PURPOSE

We didn't care what he had been, even if it was a three-time world champion. We didn't want to show him. We didn't want him to do any of his show-horse patterns or moves. We didn't need him to be famous. His bloodline did not impress us. Conversely, it would not have mattered to us if he were a pasture ornament, poorly bred, and unknown. His purpose was to tote my 10-year-old daughter around the farm and wherever else she wanted to go. He did it, with gusto. That was more important to us than titles or fame or no titles or fame. He did what we wanted him to do. And he loved it.

This is the most important thing for us to understand: God has a purpose for each of us. What-was in our lives is not as important to him as what-will-be. He is not more impressed with us if we can list many successes, or more distressed if failures underscore our name. God is not random; he is purposeful. There are things he wants us to do. Things he's planned for us to do. Things he's made us for. Let's be ready for whatever-it-is.

A verse to hang your hat on: "For I know the plans I have for you," says The Lord. "Plans for welfare and not for evil; to give you a future and a hope." – Jeremiah 29:11

Check out these verses...are you ready to be amazed?

You are:
    1. Made a certain way (hand crafted):
For you formed my inward parts; you knitted me together in my mother's womb. – Psalm 139:13
    2. For a certain number of days:
Your eyes saw my unformed substance; in your book were written, every one of them, the days that were

formed for me, when as yet there was none of them. – Psalm 139:16

  3. To live in a certain time and place:
And he made from one man every nation of mankind to live on all the face of the earth, having determined allotted periods and the boundaries of their dwelling place, – Acts 17:26

  4. To do certain things:
For we are his workmanship, created in Christ Jesus for good works, which God prepared beforehand that we should walk in them. – Ephesians 2:10

  5. For a certain reason:
In the same way, let your light so shine before others, that they may see your good works and give glory to your Father who is in heaven. – Matthew 5:16

  6. But what if God wants me to do something I don't like?
Delight yourself in the LORD, and he will give you the desires of your heart. – Psalm 37:4 (Because if you are committed to the Lord, you want the same things he wants.)

3
NOT THE PURPOSE

Regal was a 16-hand, rawboned appendix quarter horse that had worked at a kid's camp the past summer. He was a red bay with that cute, black-lined nose, like someone painted mascara just around his nostrils. He was big and quiet. He was personable, too, and looked me in the eye while I stroked his soft fur, which was woolly because it was late fall. I like a horse that's interactive. You can't communicate much to one who is always looking off somewhere. That's also a good indication of disrespect. If they're always staring off, they obviously wish they were somewhere else. Regal, however, was very interested in having me stand by him.

He loaded up perfectly on the trailer. I was pretty happy with my purchase and thinking all the way home about all the fun places I wanted to take him. Any horse that spent a summer at a kid's camp ought to like the reprieve of a single rider to read and respond to. I felt I had freed him from a place where he was just one of many horses with possibly no human attachment and was taking him to a place

NOT THE PURPOSE

where he could belong to just me and become my partner.

However, after we arrived home, he was not so interested in interaction. He would turn his tail to me and keep eating as I walked toward him in the pasture. When it was time to come in for the night, Jazz would come galloping up, but Regal wouldn't. He would come lazily, get just so close, then drive Jazz away when I went in to halter his pasture buddy. Keeping the appaloosa away threateningly, Regal would muscle in for the halter so he could go in first. After a short while, Jazz stopped running in, and they would both stay out in the big pasture--requiring us to go out and get them.

The most important rule when having horses is that the person is in charge, not the horse. Everything is more peaceable that way. But why would he think I was in charge if I wasn't doing anything about his disrespectful behavior?

One day I got him in to take him for a ride. We don't cross-tie, we just tack up in the horse's stall. Regal was standing there with his head hanging over his stall door when I went to pick up his left front foot. He gave me his foot, then seemed to think better of it. He leaned his weight into the leg and tried to pull his hoof away. When I resisted him, he acted like he was going to fall down. I knew what to do about this. I held on to the foot as he shrugged down, trying to get me to drop it. I knew he wasn't going to really fall. It was a ploy. He was shod all the way around, though, and when I jerked the foot up as he flipped his shoulder down, it produced a pretty decided whack on his elbow with his shoe. He shot up, almost clunking his head on the ceiling. I was absolutely shocked. Of course I dropped the foot. Not to be out-done, I grabbed up the foot again, but I felt his weight shift as he swung his head to bite me. I twisted out of the way but dropped the foot. It's never

NOT THE PURPOSE

good when a horse gets their way when they do something bad. That's reinforcement for bad behavior. First I lost the foot because he reared, then again when he tried to bite. I knew I was in trouble now.

We threw a halter and lead on him, and Janelle stood ready to jerk his head if he tried to bite me again. He did try. Since she was worried she wouldn't be fast enough to stop him, we cross-tied Regal. After a struggle, I cleaned his front feet all right, but he was not yielding. He kept trying to bite me even if he couldn't reach me.

This was not the purpose I had bought him for. I had had plans for him, and they did not include any of this behavior. Sure, he was happy to have me help him out of a situation he didn't like when I bought him, but as soon as he felt safe, he didn't need or want me around. He had everything he needed. Why would he want to be with me, much less obey me? I was just not an important player in his life. Sure, he liked the clean water, the grassy pasture where he grazed all day long, the clean stall at night. But why would those perks have anything to do with me? The disrespect grew and grew, especially because I did not meet the challenges as he made them. I wasn't worthy of his respect. I decided not to keep him.

How much are we like that toward God? Yeah, we want to go to heaven and all that, so we say a prayer, or think we're just as good as (or better) than the next guy so God is obligated to hold our spot for us. But what is our attitude toward him? Respect? Obedience? Attention? Or do we ignore him, shunning the thought that he's in charge, growing more disrespectful as time goes on? Every breath we take is a gift. Every good thing we have is from him. Just because he doesn't immediately punish every sin doesn't mean he doesn't take note. It just means

NOT THE PURPOSE

he's giving us time to get things figured out, before it's too late.

A verse to hang your hat on: "The Lord is not slow to fulfill his promise as some count slowness, but is patient toward you, not wishing that any should perish, but that all should reach repentance." – 2 Peter 3:9

Read about it in Deuteronomy 8:6-20.

⁶ So you shall keep the commandments of the LORD your God by walking in his ways and by fearing him. ⁷ For the LORD your God is bringing you into a good land, a land of brooks of water, of fountains and springs, flowing out in the valleys and hills, ⁸ a land of wheat and barley, of vines and fig trees and pomegranates, a land of olive trees and honey, ⁹ a land in which you will eat bread without scarcity, in which you will lack nothing, a land whose stones are iron, and out of whose hills you can dig copper. ¹⁰ And you shall eat and be full, and you shall bless the LORD your God for the good land he has given you. ¹¹ "Take care lest you forget the LORD your God by not keeping his commandments and his rules and his statutes, which I command you today, ¹² lest, when you have eaten and are full and have built good houses and live in them, ¹³ and when your herds and flocks multiply and your silver and gold is multiplied and all that you have is multiplied, ¹⁴ then your heart be lifted up, and you forget the LORD your God, who brought you out of the land of Egypt, out of the house of slavery, ¹⁵ who led you through the great and terrifying wilderness, with its fiery serpents and scorpions and thirsty ground where there was no water, who brought you water out of the flinty rock, ¹⁶ who fed you in the wilderness with manna that your fathers did not know, that he might humble you and test you, to do you good in the end.

NOT THE PURPOSE

[17]{.sup} Beware lest you say in your heart, 'My power and the might of my hand have gotten me this wealth.' [18]{.sup} You shall remember the LORD your God, for it is he who gives you power to get wealth, that he may confirm his covenant that he swore to your fathers, as it is this day. [19]{.sup} And if you forget the LORD your God and go after other gods and serve them and worship them, I solemnly warn you today that you shall surely perish. [20]{.sup} Like the nations that the LORD makes to perish before you, so shall you perish, because you would not obey the voice of the LORD your God.

4
LEAD

  Shawnee was a horse of unknown and probably mixed ancestry, but she was a very pretty golden sorrel. She was older when we got her, late teens at least, and pretty set in her ways. A comical thinking of hers was that if she could get her head through, the rest of her would fit. Sometimes the actual comical part was her surprise when she got herself stubbornly stuck between two trees on the trail because she had refused to listen to an insistent turn cue from her rider. Then she'd have to back up because she couldn't go any more forward, and she had to turn the way she should have in the first place. The real root of the problem, of course, was not listening to the rein, not just her inability to judge the size of the parts of herself behind her head.

  Another proof of her being set in her ways was where she liked to travel in a group. She didn't like to lead. If she was in front, she would zig then zag down the lane, certainly not walking forward in a straight line or with any purpose. She haltingly led, and you could tell she didn't like being first. That position much more suited Merrylegs. The Paso Fino-cross pony had seen a lot of territory in her day, and she was willing to see more. Walking slowly behind the reluctant Shawnee was not fun for her. Dixie was always willing to play fearless leader, also. In fact, not leading made her quite crazy, and Laura was working on that by sometimes holding her in the last position for nearly an entire trail ride--only when Merrylegs was leading, though. It's hard to hold back a jigging horse when the front ones are barely moving. Merrylegs and Dixie both had a get-to-town walk, especially Dixie with her Tennessee Walker gait. When Shawnee was following, she had a pretty fast walk herself, or she would jog a ways to catch up, then walk again for a while. She just wouldn't lead like that.

One day, Shawnee had an epiphany. 'Epiphany' is a fancy word for when the light bulb comes on above the head of a cartoon character. Shawnee's light bulb came on at a fun event a friend of mine planned. She urged a bunch of us to take our horses over to a local stable for some fun group riding she had planned. Always ready to try something new with friends, we loaded up Merrylegs, Shawnee, and Dixie, and headed to the stable.

One of the events my friend planned was called Trotting Races. We all lined up at one end of the arena and, you guessed it, raced at a trot for the other end. Silly as it sounds, it is incredibly easy for riders and horses in such a competition to lose sight of the goal, which was...trotting. We had all kinds of fun, since some of those races were won by the third or fourth horse to get across the line simply because they trotted the whole way and the others broke into a canter. Of course, there were calls for rematches when that happened.

Shawnee's favorite gait was the trot. It was her rider's favorite gait, too, since her canter was absolutely bone-jarring. Shawnee could trot *really fast*, and she won a few races. She actually went ahead of the other horses. She found out she liked it.

I liked it, too, and we had bragging rights for quite a while, for which she received much praise.

After the races and a break for treats for humans and equines, we mounted back up for a trail ride. I swung Shawnee in last, her favorite position. We headed out along the field next to the stable, and then made our way down the road. The horse in front of us was a slow-walking quarter horse. Shawnee was not used to walking that slow on a trail ride, and it must have been eating her. All of a sudden she picked up her pace and pulled out to pass the quarter horse. I didn't stop her. I was amazed and delighted that Shawnee, on her own, wanted to be in front of another horse. She didn't pull back in behind the next horse up, either. She stayed on her quick-walking course and passed five horses, including Merrylegs. She started jogging her catch-up jog, and moved to the front of the group. I couldn't believe it. Ears pricked and in completely new territory, my little last-position horse had solidly claimed leadership.

A few days later Janelle and I went for a ride in the woods next to our creek. Janelle led out on Merrylegs, and Shawnee and I happily followed. Janelle and I chatted as we headed to the back of the woods, the horses stepping out briskly. When we reached the ditch behind the woods, Janelle decided to cross it instead of traveling all the way to the bridge. She pulled up and faced Merrylegs at it. The usually so forward-thinking pony danced a little reluctant jig. Shawnee suddenly started forward, and I urged her on. She brushed past Merrylegs and calmly stepped down into the ditch and back up the other side. She didn't hesitate to wait for her comrade to resume primacy. She stepped out boldly on the trail with no zig-zagging or reluctant steps. I was ecstatic.

Shawnee was a leader.

LEAD

All of us assume a position when we're in a group. A lot of personality and circumstantial factors usually go into our choosing a safe place to travel in a crowd. Although not everyone's a natural-born leader, leadership can be a choice we make. Sometimes it's scary to lead because we don't really know where we're going, either. But when it comes to God's Word and right and wrong, we must be ready to step up. We can't be the one following the group, or even somewhere in the middle joining in. We are called to lead, even if that means stepping out alone. But here's the thing: even if someone else would not lead, if they see a leader going the way they really wanted to but wouldn't dare by themselves, they will join. Shawnee always did that. She was a willing follower. But then she became a confident leader, not even caring if her buddy followed because she knew she was doing the right thing. That's what we need to do. We can't be afraid to lead in doing right, because others need a leader to follow.

A verse to hang your hat on: "Let the LORD, the God of the spirits of all flesh, appoint a man over the congregation who shall go out before them and come in before them, who shall lead them out and bring them in, that the congregation of the LORD may not be as sheep that have no shepherd." – Numbers 27:16, 17

Read about it in Titus 2:1-15.

¹ But as for you, teach what accords with sound doctrine. ² Older men are to be sober-minded, dignified, self-controlled, sound in faith, in love, and in steadfastness.³ Older women likewise are to be reverent in behavior, not slanderers or slaves to much wine. They are to teach what is good, ⁴ and so train the young women to love their husbands and children, ⁵ to be self-controlled, pure, working at home, kind, and submissive to their own husbands, that the word of God may not be reviled. ⁶ Likewise, urge the younger men to be self-controlled. ⁷ Show yourself in all respects to be a model of good works, and in your teaching show integrity, dignity, ⁸ and sound speech that cannot be condemned, so that an opponent may be put to shame, having nothing evil to say about us. ⁹ Slaves are to be submissive to their own masters in everything; they are to be well-pleasing, not argumentative, ¹⁰ not pilfering, but showing all good faith, so that in everything they may adorn the doctrine of God our Savior. ¹¹ For the grace of God has appeared, bringing salvation for all people, ¹² training us to renounce ungodliness and worldly passions, and to live self-controlled, upright, and godly lives in the present age, ¹³ waiting for our blessed hope, the appearing of the glory of our great God and Savior Jesus Christ, ¹⁴ who gave himself for us to redeem us from all lawlessness and to purify for himself a people for his own possession who are zealous for good works. ¹⁵ Declare these things; exhort and rebuke with all authority. Let no one disregard you.

5
COPY THAT

Here's a tip. When you go to buy a horse, try it out by doing the thing you plan on doing with it. If you're going to ride it in a pen, do some laps in a pen. If you're going to run barrels, run some. And if you plan on riding trail, at least take the horse down the driveway. I know that may sound absolutely basic to you, and good for you. But I wish someone would have said that straight out to me, nice and clear like that, so I couldn't forget it. Now we just shorten it to, "If you don't try 'em, don't buy 'em". Has a ring to it.

Before the rhyme, we managed to shake the foundations of common sense by purchasing a 14-hand POA (Pony Of the Americas) named Coke. Instead of riding him, or even leading him, away from the barn, as a smart trail rider looking for a trail horse would do, we had Janelle ride him in the little paddock behind the barn herding sheep. Oh, yes, they had a great time cutting the sheep and driving them to various corners of the paddock. Coke seemed to be in tune to Janelle's every cue as they cavorted after the thoroughly confused woollies. There was not a buck, a head toss, nothing that would indicate anything but a pony that was compliant and easy for a twelve-year-old girl to handle. The owners weren't asking an arm and a leg for him, either, so we bought him. They even mentioned that he didn't really like to be off in his own too much, but we figured we could cure him of that.

We gave him some transition time, getting him familiar across the fence line with Jazz and Widget, getting him used to us and our trails. We let a week pass before tacking Coke up. After bringing him in and brushing him, we fussed with finding a good-fitting bit for him and making sure we had his saddle padded comfortably. It took a while, this fussing, and he was not thrilled at being the only one in the barn. We weren't too concerned. He didn't know about us yet, so we were deliberate and kind, using the situation to help him know he could trust us.

Finally, we led him out. He burst out of the barn and got an eye on the other two horses, ignoring us. Not the same attitude we had experienced at his previous residence, and we weren't too enthusiastic about it. Our plan was to ride near the pasture today, though, and since his owners said he was a little reluctant to go off by himself, we weren't going to try anything like that. We knew how to alleviate horsey fears. Start out close and work yourself away, then back, repeat. Once they get the idea they're coming back, they get a lot more cooperative about going away. The key was to turn them before they threw a fit, so it wasn't like you were giving in to a tantrum. That would be teaching the horse to throw a tantrum when they weren't happy, which would be a very foolish thing teach indeed.

Janelle mounted up. Coke was so intently watching Jazz and Widget standing at the fence he didn't seem to notice. That boded no good, so I stuck close. Janelle gathered the reins and squeezed. Coke took two steps. He stopped. He reared. It wasn't a vertical rear, but it wasn't a little hop, either. Janelle leaned forward, I sprang to Coke's head, and he reared again. Thoroughly aghast and more than a little irritated, I grabbed the rein nearest me and pulled him down. He took two steps forward and went up again. What was the matter with this horse? We were walking, or rather, rearing, our way toward the other horses, not away. He wasn't like this at all when we tried him out. I pulled him down and forward. This time he walked at least five feet before he reared. So strange. Just stop, rear, come down, rear. No bucking, head shaking, running out, pulling away. Just rear, stop, rear.

"Maybe it's the saddle," I said. "You rode him with theirs. Maybe ours is pinching him."

Like a good sport, Janelle hopped off and stripped the saddle and pad off the gelding. He stood quiet. I gave her a leg up and led him forward. Up he went again. Bareback and up is a little more interesting than with a saddle. Janelle grabbed his mane and leaned forward, and I yanked at his bit. He took two more steps and went up again. When his front feet hit the ground, Janelle slid off. She never rode him again.

I spent some time on the phone with the previous owners, who said he never reared at their place and I must be feeding him too much sweet feed. I don't feed sweet feed, and I only feed enough pellets to get vitamins in my horses, something like a one-cup serving. I called a cowboy trainer friend of mine. He didn't have much to offer me, other than some scary stories and a training trick that worked for him but involved riding I was not advanced enough to do. Trying to re-train a rearing horse without getting hurt was above my pay grade. I knew people who ended up with a smashed pelvis and other broken bones because their horse reared up came over backward on them.

I fussed and fumed about what to do. I finally decided to try a tie-down. I figured if he couldn't get his nose up high enough to get the lift for a rear, his plan would be foiled and he would give up. (I didn't know that tie downs work for horses that bolt, but can be a danger to use for one that rears.) I fitted a tie down between the loop on the cinch and Coke's chin strap. We tacked up Jazz, too. Maybe if we had both horses out and took a ride together, he'd quit that rearing business. It seemed to work, too. I got on Coke, and Janelle led the way to the driveway on Jazz. I was just feeling a little less tense and a little more confident, when all of a sudden I felt that little POA gather himself under me. I grabbed for his left rein and pulled some leather, forcing his rear to become a half turn. He did not like that, and bowed his neck, shoving his nose up, down and back. I lost tension on the rein, and since I was leaning so hard into it, I found myself sprawled on the ground. From that vantage point, I watched Coke take a few steps away then rear. The tie-down stretched tight. The gelding couldn't get his balance. He tried to counter himself and ended up rearing higher, taking a couple awkward steps--and over backward he went!

But it wasn't over yet.

A couple of days later, Janelle wanted to go for a ride, so we tacked up Jazz and headed out, her riding and me walking. We were looking forward to a good time out on the trails and were talking and laughing cheerily. We got up to the spot where Coke had thrown himself over backward...and Jazz reared.

Learned behavior. One of the best ways to learn something is to be with someone doing it. Watching how they do it and mimicking their movements makes the thing easier for us to pick up. Sometimes I find myself saying weird words because a friend does. Sometimes I don't even like the words, but I say them, anyway! We pick up gestures, sayings, and ideas. Ideas--the way we think and process information--comprise the most powerful influence on our lives because what we *do* is driven by what we *think*. Who and what is making that kind of impact on us? Who will we give the authority to mold our thinking?

A verse to hang your hat on: "Therefore be imitators of God, as beloved children." – Ephesians 5:1

Read about it in Romans 12:1-21.

[1] I appeal to you therefore, brothers, by the mercies of God, to present your bodies as a living sacrifice, holy and acceptable to God, which is your spiritual worship. [2] Do not be conformed to this world, but be transformed by the renewal of your mind, that by testing you may discern what is the will of God, what is good and acceptable and perfect.[3] For by the grace given to me I say to everyone among you not to think of himself more highly than he ought to think, but to think with sober judgment, each according to the measure of faith that God has assigned. [4] For as in one body we have many members, and the members do not all have the same function, [5] so we, though many, are one body in Christ, and individually members one of another. [6] Having gifts that differ according to the grace given to us, let us use them: if prophecy, in proportion to our faith; [7] if service, in our serving; the one who teaches, in his teaching; [8] the one who exhorts, in his exhortation; the one who contributes, in generosity; the one who leads, with zeal; the one who does acts of mercy, with cheerfulness.[9] Let love be genuine. Abhor what is evil; hold fast to what is good. [10] Love one another with

brotherly affection. Outdo one another in showing honor. ⁱⁱ Do not be slothful in zeal, be fervent in spirit, serve the Lord. ¹² Rejoice in hope, be patient in tribulation, be constant in prayer. ¹³ Contribute to the needs of the saints and seek to show hospitality. ¹⁴ Bless those who persecute you; bless and do not curse them. ¹⁵ Rejoice with those who rejoice, weep with those who weep. ¹⁶ Live in harmony with one another. Do not be haughty, but associate with the lowly. Never be wise in your own sight. ¹⁷ Repay no one evil for evil, but give thought to do what is honorable in the sight of all. ¹⁸ If possible, so far as it depends on you, live peaceably with all. ¹⁹ Beloved, never avenge yourselves, but leave it to the wrath of God, for it is written, "Vengeance is mine, I will repay, says the Lord." ²⁰ To the contrary, "if your enemy is hungry, feed him; if he is thirsty, give him something to drink; for by so doing you will heap burning coals on his head." ²¹ Do not be overcome by evil, but overcome evil with good.

6
FENCED IN

After you've had a horse for a while, you kind of get this trust thing built up with them. One of the things we did with that trust was to let Shawnee eat grass around the barn. We didn't have to tie her to anything. We would leave her out after a ride, or call her in from the pasture if we were working around the barn. We would throw a halter on her and make a low sweep with an arm like a glamorous hostess on a game show and say, "Do you want to eat?" We only did that motion and said those words when we wanted a horse to eat. I've been on the other end of a lead rope attached to a pony who was constantly diving his head and stopping when I was trying to take him somewhere. When I grew up and gained the proper training knowledge, I found out a horse can quickly learn the disadvantages of that kind of behavior. I benefited from their learning: no more feeling like my arms were being jerked out of the sockets. Discipline creates pleasantness. It also allows you to spoil your horse with the long grass around the barn.

FENCED IN

One day after a ride, I led Shawnee out into the hayfield behind the barn and let her eat out there. I had decided to fence in the part of it that extended like the tail of the letter "P" next to the barn. I figured she may as well eat while I pounded stakes.

I stood and estimated the number of posts I would need. Four for the corners, three down each short side, five down each long side. I started gathering T-posts from my stash and carrying them over to the corners in loads of four. Shawnee ate. I rummaged around in the barn for my lovely braided wire which I had wound back onto the spool when I took down the last temporary pasture. Shawnee ate. I brought the spool and the bag of insulators out to the intended corner closest to the barn. Shawnee ate. I went back to the barn for the post pounder, then proceeded to pound in the four corner posts. Shawnee ate.

I clipped a couple of insulators to the first corner post, made a loop in the wire to hold it onto one of them, and started walking the spool toward the next corner, probably seventy-five feet away. Now, my husband is one of those guys that could pound in a hundred posts and they would all be in a straight line. He has a good eye for that. I...do not. I cheat. I string the wire all the way around the pasture on just the four corners, then I pound in the intermediate posts to match where the wire is.

I pounded in the post at the second corner, clipped insulators, threaded my wire through one and headed to the next corner. I pounded the post and pulled the wire tight on the insulator. Shawnee was still eating, not having moved very far from where I had first released her. She was maybe thirty feet away, almost knee-deep in grass, happily watching me. I said some inane thing to her about making a pasture for her. I picked up the spool and

FENCED IN

started walking forward to close the last side of the pasture, my wire unspooling behind me.

Before I got ten feet, Shawnee picked up her head and walked purposefully *into* the unfinished pasture. About twenty feet inside, she dropped her head again and happily went back to eating. I stopped. I could not believe my eyes. She had pastured herself? While she had the whole hayfield to be in, she chose the little piece of it I had sectioned off?

I finished walking my wire to the last corner post and attached an insulated handle for a gate. Shawnee ate. I pounded in the rest of the posts, making nice straight sides. Shawnee ate. I got the extension cord out of the garage and pulled the fencer down from the hanger in the barn, installing them to electrify the fence. I stood back and wondered why I needed to do that. It wasn't like she was going to try to get out. I watched Shawnee eat. I went to her and she lifted her head so I could take off her halter. Then she ate. Every line of her spelled happy horsey. I walked back to the barn to hang up her halter shaking my head at my content-to-be-fenced-in mare.

God gives people lots of boundaries. The Bible calls them laws, statutes, his word, precepts, decrees, commands. We call them rules. Most often we aren't fond of rules. We feel constricted and bound, more at war with the rules than at peace with them. I never really looked at God's boundaries like fences. Fences keep horses safe. It's a big world out there, full of dangers--like traffic on the highway and people that might not return them to where they belong. A horse can do anything horses like to do inside a fence. Run. Play. Sleep. Eat. It's just that all those things can be done in safety.

I want to be like Shawnee. Even if I could be out-there, away from God's boundaries, I'd rather be in-there, where there is all kinds of freedom, but also protection. To be outside God's protection is a very scary thought indeed.

A verse to hang your hat on: "I say to the LORD, 'You are my Lord; I have no good apart from you.'" – Psalm 16:1

Read more about it in Deuteronomy 4:1-8.

¹ "And now, O Israel, listen to the statutes and the rules that I am teaching you, and do them, that you may live, and go in and take possession of the land that the LORD, the God of your fathers, is giving you. ² You shall not add to the word that I command you, nor take from it, that you may keep the commandments of the LORD your God that I command you. ³ Your eyes have seen what the LORD did at Baal-peor, for the LORD your God destroyed from among you all the men who followed the Baal of Peor. ⁴ But you who held fast to the LORD your God are all alive today.⁵ See, I have taught you statutes and rules, as the LORD my God commanded me, that you should do them in the land that you are entering to take possession of it. ⁶ Keep them and do them, for that will be your wisdom and your understanding in the sight of the peoples, who, when they hear all these statutes, will say, 'Surely this great nation is a wise and understanding people.' ⁷ For what great nation is there that has a god so near to it as the LORD our God is to us, whenever we call upon him? ⁸ And what great nation is there, that has statutes and rules so righteous as all this law that I set before you today?

7
NOT A SUGGESTION

When we sold the house we lived in so we could move out to the farm, there was some lag time between the selling and the availability of the new house. We had started construction earlier in the spring, and we hoped to be in by fall. Most people rent a storage unit for their things in a local lock-n-store facility I suppose, but we aren't most people. We knew the between-time was going to span several months, and, though we tried not to be hoarders, we had lots of stuff. Not only house stuff, furniture, and clothes, but also Wayne's considerable stash of tools and equipment. Since the size we needed for a unit at the lock-n-store seemed cost-prohibitive, we bought a forty-eight-foot semi trailer. Our neighbor was a trucker. He kindly went to get it, and, when we had packed it to the gills, he brought it over to the farm and parked it a safe bit away from the construction zone. When we emptied the semi trailer and moved into our house and shop months later, we kept it. We hauled it to a rather inconspicuous place by the woods along the creek. Wayne built a dirt ramp up to the back door and made kind of a nice dirt berm with a gentle slope next to it to veil the running gear, and we used it as a storage barn. At this point you're probably thinking you didn't need to know all that, or maybe you're wondering how redneck a family can be. However, this semi box is an important player in a situation that happened one fall day about eight years later.

My friend Marcia came over to ride. Janelle came out with us, and we collected Shawnee, Merrylegs, and Dixie and turned them into their stalls for a treat and tacking up. The mares were pretty glad to munch on their handful of grain as we brushed them then cinched on their saddles. We started up the lane next to the hayfield with Merrylegs leading. I had a large section of the hayfield fenced in, ready for winter pasture. When the ground gets hard and snow lies deep, the horses spend the greater part of winter keeping themselves warm by digging for the fetlock-deep grass. Right now, though, they had to stay in the torn-up dirt pen, and hay was all they got. Our land is low and heavy. If it's a wet season, they tear it up really quick. Since a torn-up hayfield does not yield well and is miserable to drive a tractor over, the horses had to wait for a good frost to hit before we could start using it.

There was a high, dry area behind the hayfield pasture that I left open for riding. We made our way to it and rode around some, trotting circles and figure eights. Marcia had never ridden Dixie before, and it's always good policy to let a person and horse get used to each other in a somewhat controlled environment. I grow weary of compulsory movements quite quickly, however, so I pulled Shawnee toward the lane and put her in a canter to do a wide circle in the whole area instead of those stinkery, precise movements.

Evidently, Shawnee agreed with my decision to head south, back to the barn, but my guidance to

NOT A SUGGESTION

the west seemed to take her by surprise, or rather, disagreed with her. She did a weave-jerk to stay on the lane, and my knees and insistent hands barely got the right turn we needed to miss the corner post of the fence and head west. Angry at being thwarted, Shawnee leaped to a bone-jarring gallop, rocketing toward the creek, its woods--and the semi trailer.

Irritation quickly took a shortcut to near-panic when my strong pull on the right rein only caused her to turn her head at about a ninety-degree angle, so she was looking straight north and running straight west. I kept her head bent and put my back into it as we thundered ever closer to that semi box. I yelled and kicked her left side furiously with no influence on her speed or direction. She stared at me out of her right eye, and the look in it was not upset or fearful or flustered--it was determined. With the fence speeding by on the left and the semi box imminently ahead, I contemplated bailing off. Her staring at me out of her right eye was scaring me. Could she see the semi box looming in front of us with her other eye? What was she thinking? *Was* she thinking? No good thing could come from us hitting that box at this speed.

There was one other option. There was an opening to shoot for between the corner fence post and the front of the semi trailer. I held her head solid to the right, but zipped my left hand up on the left rein. Then I hunkered down, gripping tightly with both knees. My heart pounded as I waited the split seconds to the last corner post. Alongside the last post, I let loose with my right hand. I grabbed that left rein tight and pulled leather. Her braced neck shot left with all her resistance behind it as well as my adrenalized insistence. She pivoted around that pole, lucky to keep her feet, and jarred to a halt.

I'm not ashamed to say I was shaking like a leaf. I slung her around and trotted her back to

NOT A SUGGESTION

Marcia and Janelle, who were still standing dumbfounded where we left them. Shawnee meekly obeyed.

"I thought she was going to run right into that semi box!" Marcia exploded. "I couldn't believe she was running straight toward it even though you had her head turned completely sideways!"

"She was looking right at me," I responded angrily. "If she was thinking anything, it was 'ain't gonna'. She could have killed us!"

I remember the feeling of anger, fear, and disappointment all mixed up inside me. Add adrenaline to that, and you can imagine that I wasn't going to be giving her much free rein. What a stupid stunt! Sure, my plan was a different than hers and she got a little annoyed. But what a crazy plan it was to resist me to the point of possible injury! My commands were in her self-interest. Those stinkery, concise motions we were doing at first were to teach her to bend to my guidance. They would consistently hone her into a mature, steady, useful mount. If she had just done what I asked, there would have been peace, praise, and reward. My insistent commands when she got to running away would have turned her from impending disaster. My last-ditch effort was most likely uncomfortable, judging from her surprised, awkward, stop. I don't even think she saw that semi box until we turned, and I bet she was startled by how close a call it had been.

My question is this: when do we come to realize that God's commands aren't suggestions? They can't be. Some are for teaching us to be mature and useful. That's the commands that start out, "Do this..." Some snatch us away from behavior that would destroy us. Those are the ones that start out, "Don't do that..." All of God's commands are for our good. We can't ignore any of them!

NOT A SUGGESTION

A verse to hang your hat on: "All Scripture is breathed out by God and profitable for teaching, for reproof, for correction, and for training in righteousness, that the man of God may be complete, equipped for every good work." – Timothy 3:16, 17

Read about it in Psalm 19: 7-14.

7 The law of the LORD is perfect, reviving the soul; the testimony of the LORD is sure, making wise the simple; 8 the precepts of the LORD are right, rejoicing the heart; the commandment of the LORD is pure, enlightening the eyes; 9 the fear of the LORD is clean, enduring forever; the rules of the LORD are true, and righteous altogether. 10 More to be desired are they than gold, even much fine gold; sweeter also than honey and drippings of the honeycomb. 11 Moreover, by them is your servant warned; in keeping them there is great reward. 12 Who can discern his errors? Declare me innocent from hidden faults. 13 Keep back your servant also from presumptuous sins; let them not have dominion over me! Then I shall be blameless, and innocent of great transgression. 14 Let the words of my mouth and the meditation of my heart be acceptable in your sight, O LORD, my rock and my redeemer.

8
REST

When it comes to horses that can't stand still, I don't care for pawing, or head dipping, or bit-lipping (especially when a bit-lipper gets the rein and starts sucking on it or grinding it between their teeth), or the naughty equine who sneaks a nip at my toe. None of those was Skipper's reaction to inactivity. She just couldn't keep her feet still. Maybe it was because whenever I was with Skipper, we were always doing something, so of course standing around seemed odd to her. Oh, she could stand for a minute or two, but then shuffle, shuffle, shuffle. I'd lift the reins and tell her briskly to "hoh", and she would stop. For a minute. Usually, I didn't mind, because she and I had places to go. When I rode, I liked to hit the road, and standing around was a waste of the valuable time I had to rob from something else.

However, a day always comes when that one thing that's not a big deal becomes a big deal. Skipper and I were competing in a Judged Trail Ride. That's a fun little deal the Tennessee Walking Horse Association around here puts on in May every year for horses of every breed. It's held at a part of the state forest designated for trail riding. The Ride has 10 stations situated at random on about 10 miles of winding trails. Each station is set up to test a horse's trust in the rider. All manner of scary things were involved, such as picking up a towel out of a laundry basket, zigzagging between three or four tents up to the clothesline, and hanging the towel, all while mounted. Sometimes the obstacle included walking between balloons, or carrying a bunch of balloons from one place to another, or walking on tarps or black-painted plywood sheets, or shooting a basketball from horseback. The completion of each task was judged from one to ten. At the end of the day, everyone turned in their scorecards, the scores were added up, and a big ceremony with cash prizes and ribbons was held to honor the horse and rider with the highest score.

Our little problem came to a head at the elephant box. Yes, I mean the one where the elephant stands on a little box, all four feet jammed together. The thing about the Judged Trail Ride is that every year the tasks change, and you have no idea what they are until you encounter them. Therefore, there is no practicing. Communication and try are the key. Since no one has practiced, the judges give contestants three tries or a certain length of time to accomplish the obstacle. Consequently, traffic backs up at difficult assignments.

The trail leading to the elephant box trial was narrow and shaded, thank goodness, because the line was long. The box was in a little clearing ahead. Horses waited in single file, which made passing the time in conversation difficult. The closest trees were sassafras, and since horses don't care for that flavor, they were bored. When we stopped, there were four horses ahead of us and more pulled in behind us. The underbrush was so thick we couldn't see the horse and rider working on the box.

Skipper started shifting on the trail while I was talking to my friend in front of us. Her horse stood hip shot, probably glad for the break. We had already traveled a good three miles, but Skipper didn't seem to share the gelding's welcome of rest. When I turned in the saddle to talk to the woman behind me, Skipper tried to pivot on the trail. She backed into a sapling and got her head stuck in a bush. Yeah, it was funny then, too.

By the time we were second in line, standing on the edge of the clearing watching the horse and rider attempt the elephant box, Skipper was done simply shuffling and shifting. She wanted to get moving. My efforts to hold her in place were not met with grace. She backed and turned. Her efforts to move around were not met with grace from me. I thought her jigging was detrimental to the horse trying to figure out the elephant box, and that was not fair to them. Sideways we went for three or four big steps. Finally, I turned her around and faced the trail full of waiting horses. She seemed stumped. There was no room on that trail to get by! In her contemplation of how to negotiate the trail with no room, she stood still for a bit. Frustrated, she made to turn around again, jigged sideways, and wound up with her face in the underbrush again. I didn't get a chance to see my friend and her horse attempt the box. I had to ask her how they did later.

Finally, it was our turn. I walked Skipper up to the box and told her to touch it. She shoved her nose at the box and plunked it down on top. I said, "Step up," which is what I say when she gets to the back of the trailer. She pawed at the box and danced around it to the left. I straightened her back out and asked her again. The hollow thudding of her pawing hoof on the box echoed in the clearing. Skipper put a front foot on it. I asked her to step up again, and she put her other front foot up there. They were too close to the near side of the box for her to get her back feet on. Hoping she'd step forward, I said, "Hop in", which is what I say right after "step up" to get her to hop into the trailer. She stood still a moment, thinking, and I said "Hop in" again. I felt her gather herself, dropping down just a little like a depressed spring...and she jumped over the box. It was a move just like leap-frog. Although I thought it was more spectacular than standing on the box, and enthusiastically praised Skipper for such a huge effort...the judge did not. We did not get points for improvisation. Which is fair, after all. We didn't accomplish the task.

I wondered if Skips had just been less wound up, if she could have rested and been calm when we approached the box, would she have figured out what I wanted her to do instead of just throwing herself over it with all that bottled energy? Her impatience made it hard for me to do anything but resist her, which made her more upset. It also made it hard for me to communicate with her. I just wanted her to rest and be content. With me, not against me.

Rest. How much we do that? Do we take time out, not just to sleep or nap, but to stop in our endeavors, to stop pushing forward, to stop working, to stop doing? God gave us one day a week, as a gift, when he wants us to rest. We need it to re-balance ourselves, to remember that God has things for us to do. His plan was that we would put aside time for him, to communicate with him in an intentional way. Nothing calms us down like remembering everything belongs to him and he has everything under control. Do we take him up on it? Or do we spend that day busily moving, ignoring him and his provision? When we feel like we're going nowhere, being resisted at every turn, and maybe even stuck, God invites us to rest and intentionally concentrate on him.

REST

Verses to hang your hat on: "Remember the Sabbath day, to keep it holy. Six days you shall labor, and do all your work, but the seventh day is a Sabbath to the LORD your God. On it you shall not do any work, you, or your son, or your daughter, your male servant, or your female servant, or your livestock, or the sojourner who is within your gates. For in six days the LORD made heaven and earth, the sea, and all that is in them, and rested on the seventh day. Therefore the LORD blessed the Sabbath day and made it holy." – Exodus 20:8-11

Read about it in Psalm 121.

[1] I lift up my eyes to the hills. From where does my help come? [2] My help comes from the LORD, who made heaven and earth. [3] He will not let your foot be moved; he who keeps you will not slumber. [4] Behold, he who keeps Israel will neither slumber nor sleep. [5] The LORD is your keeper; the LORD is your shade on your right hand. [6] The sun shall not strike you by day, nor the moon by night. [7] The LORD will keep you from all evil; he will keep your life. [8] The LORD will keep your going out and your coming in from this time forth and forevermore.

9
OWNING IT

Stormy was born during the night, and during--you guessed it--a storm. To be fair, she wasn't supposed to be born until August according to the last vet check, and it was only June 21. We almost named the little palomino filly Summer, since she was born on the first day of summer, but it didn't take long, only a couple of hours, to know why Stormy suited her much better.

I had bought Stormy's mom, Tasha, about four months earlier. She was a dark sorrel pony, kind of like rusty water. What I liked about her when I first saw her was that the kid riding her couldn't get her to move. His big pony kicks to her sides made her grunt but didn't have much effect on her feet. I know that sounds like a silly thing to like, but I had two boys, five and seven years old, that I wanted to introduce to the world of horses with a kind, slow pony. I planned on leading them around on her for a while, and let them get the hang of riding. By the time they knew what they were doing, so would she.

Tasha was very fat, I admit, and my husband questioned whether she might be in foal, but I was pretty sure she was just a good eater and probably stood by a round bale all day. My husband was right (as usual), and she kept getting fatter. The vet concurred. So I was pretty excited, seeing as this would be the first horse born on my farm!

After the initial shock of seeing the foal curled up by Tasha's feet that morning, I trotted back to the barn to grab a halter. I knew it was important to handle a baby the first day and start socializing it to humans right away. They call it imprinting. But when Tasha saw the halter in my hand, she ran away. Unusual for her, and it was not a good first impression for the baby. I kind of cornered them, and Tasha let me come right up to her, which was normal. But the baby skittered away, having come to the conclusion in a hurry that close contact was bad. I led Tasha out of the pasture, but the filly did not stay tucked to her side like a normal baby. She lagged behind, which made Tasha nervous. It was even trickier when I led Tasha into the barn. Because Stormy was trotting sporadically all over the yard and then balked at coming in the barn, I had to tie Tasha in the stall, leave the stall door open, and half-shoo the baby in. More bad impressions.

The boys were excited to see the new baby, but she made sure to tuck herself on the other side of her momma at all times. I had Nathan lean against the corner of the stall, telling him she would get curious after a while, like foals are, and she would come check him out. I was busy brushing Tasha, who was loving the attention, the stall, and the hay I hung in the corner. I was ignoring the baby, trying to make her feel safe by watching her mom enjoy being by me. But everything I knew and had read about babies seemed to not apply to Stormy. She got quite fed up with our presence, and instead of curiously checking Nathan out, she rounded Tasha, threw a kick at him that almost landed on his face, and dived back under her mom's neck. If I tried to touch her back, she would start bucking and dart to the other side of Tasha. I knew I was in trouble.

I called the vet and asked what to do. She said to lay Stormy down and not let her up until she was done struggling. This exercise would impress dominance on the disrespectful baby. I followed her directions with care. I laid the struggling foal down on her side and kept her down. She tried once to get up...and then she fell asleep! Not kidding. Eyes closed, legs limp. No struggling. She just shut me out. I called the vet and reported this strange behavior. She said, "You're in trouble."

Now you know why Stormy was named Stormy.

I kept them stalled a couple of days to try to get Stormy used to us. We spent a lot of time in the barn with them. Tasha was loving the attention and seemed almost giddy with the fact that she had a baby. She never was bothered by my often-thwarted efforts to touch her baby, and she never seemed upset by a thing I did. Her serenity did not rub off on Stormy, who was determined that we would not befriend her. The third morning, I led Tasha out of the stall toward the pasture, figuring on getting them in that evening. Stormy refused to follow Tasha. Even though Tasha called, Stormy trekked all over the yard. Tasha got all kinds of upset when I tried to get her to the pasture. Enough of that. Back to the stall we went, with another session of shooing Stormy in. Consequently, Stormy got halter-broke on day three.

I made a rope halter out of thick cotton clothesline. Since she was a pony baby, I needed a really small halter, and I was pretty sure it would be hard to find one. I knew a rope halter was the way to go because I needed all the control I could get. Getting the halter on her was a trick since standing by me was not a priority on her agenda. She got the hang of the halter pretty quickly, but the victory was bitter-sweet. I could lead her to the pasture all right, but then what? I didn't dare leave it on her while she was in the pasture. She might get a foot stuck in it since rope halters do not fit snugly. I had to take it off and watch her trot away.

Janelle came with me when it was time to put them in. Tasha came happily to the gate and stuffed her nose in the halter. She knew a lovely bit of grain awaited her in the barn. Stormy, however, had no such inkling of good. She only had memories of me shooing her around and, most recently, of me pulling on her head and making her walk way too close to me. She played her little "can't catch me" game around Tasha, then took off on her spindly legs in a stiff-legged canter toward the back of the pasture. As was my wont, I dogged her. Of course I had not round-penned this three-day-old baby, so she had no idea what she was in for. I knew what I was in for: a workout. This was a large pasture to be chasing a horse in. My salvation was that she didn't want to get too far from Tasha. Her self-sufficiency was starting to slip. She didn't expect me to chase her, and she was beginning to get a little freaked out. I wouldn't let her get near her mom. I would cut her off as she ran in, and change her direction. Tasha seemed to know what I was up to, and she stood nicely next to Janelle and waited. I was glad she didn't add a bunch of drama to the situation. There was already enough of that. Stormy started whinnying as she ran, but Tasha didn't answer. I kept turning her away, waiting for her to stop and face me, which meant she was giving up. Instead, she seemed to be getting more upset and running more frantically, while I was getting out of breath. Just when I was afraid she would never quit, Stormy whirled around on her umteenth trip to the back of the pasture, maybe thirty feet ahead of me. I stopped dead in my tracks and rocked back on my heels.

OWNING IT

After a few seconds of stand-off, I turned and started walking back to Tasha. A very humble Stormy followed. We waited for her at the gate. When she walked up and stopped at Tasha's side, I stepped over to her and slid the halter on her head. She stood still, puffing, while I tied it, and stuck next to Tasha as we walked to the barn.

I must say that was not the last time I had trouble catching her, but every time she gave in quicker, and soon she was putting her nose in the loop of the rope halter. She had learned she had to come to me, and she couldn't depend on hiding behind her mother to get where she wanted to go. She had to come to terms with me herself.

Sooner or later everyone has to come to that conclusion. When it comes to Jesus, we can't hide behind our parents or what someone else has done for us. Sure, when we were little, they may have taken us to church, sent us to Sunday School and youth group, had us baptized, or made us go to vacation Bible school or after-school Bible study. And good for them. But that's not good enough for God. We have to come to him ourselves and have a relationship with him that's all our very own.

A verse to hang your hat on: "If you confess with your mouth that Jesus is Lord, and believe in your heart that God has raised him from the dead, you will be saved." – Romans 10:9

Read about it in John 4:7-42.

[7] A woman from Samaria came to draw water. Jesus said to her, "Give me a drink." [8] (For his disciples had gone away into the city to buy food.) [9] The Samaritan woman said to him, "How is it that you, a Jew, ask for a drink from me, a woman of Samaria?" (For Jews have no dealings with Samaritans.) [10] Jesus answered her, "If you knew the gift of God, and who it

is that is saying to you, 'Give me a drink,' you would have asked him, and he would have given you living water." [11] The woman said to him, "Sir, you have nothing to draw water with, and the well is deep. Where do you get that living water? [12] Are you greater than our father Jacob? He gave us the well and drank from it himself, as did his sons and his livestock." [13] Jesus said to her, "Everyone who drinks of this water will be thirsty again, [14] but whoever drinks of the water that I will give him will never be thirsty again. The water that I will give him will become in him a spring of water welling up to eternal life." [15] The woman said to him, "Sir, give me this water, so that I will not be thirsty or have to come here to draw water." [16] Jesus said to her, "Go, call your husband, and come here." [17] The woman answered him, "I have no husband." Jesus said to her, "You are right in saying, 'I have no husband'; [18] for you have had five husbands, and the one you now have is not your husband. What you have said is true." [19] The woman said to him, "Sir, I perceive that you are a prophet. [20] Our fathers worshiped on this mountain, but you say that in Jerusalem is the place where people ought to worship." [21] Jesus said to her, "Woman, believe me, the hour is coming when neither on this mountain nor in Jerusalem will you worship the Father. [22] You worship what you do not know; we worship what we know, for salvation is from the Jews. [23] But the hour is coming, and is now here, when the true worshipers will worship the Father in spirit and truth, for the Father is seeking such people to worship him. [24] God is spirit, and those who worship him must worship in spirit and truth." [25] The woman said to him, "I know that Messiah is coming (he who is called Christ). When he comes, he will tell us all things." [26] Jesus said to her, "I who speak to you am he." [27] Just then his disciples came back. They marveled that he was talking with a woman, but no *one said, "What do you seek?" or, "Why are you talking with her?" ²⁸ So the woman left her water jar and went away into town and said to the people, ²⁹ "Come, see a man who told me all that I ever did. Can this be the Christ?" ³⁰ They went out of the town and were coming to him. ³¹ Meanwhile the disciples were urging him, saying, "Rabbi, eat." ³² But he said to them, "I have food to eat that you do not know about." ³³ So the disciples said to one another, "Has anyone brought him something to eat?" ³⁴ Jesus said to them, "My food is to do the will of him who sent me and to accomplish his work. ³⁵ Do you not say, 'There are yet four months, then comes the harvest'? Look, I tell you, lift up your eyes, and see that the fields are white for harvest. ³⁶ Already the one who reaps is receiving wages and gathering fruit for eternal life, so that sower and reaper may rejoice together. ³⁷ For here the saying holds true, 'One sows and another reaps.' ³⁸ I sent you to reap that for which you did not labor. Others have labored, and you have entered into their labor." ³⁹ Many Samaritans from that town believed in him because of the woman's testimony, "He told me all that I ever did." ⁴⁰ So when the Samaritans came to him, they asked him to stay with them, and he stayed there two days. ⁴¹ And many more believed because of his word. ⁴² They said to the woman, "It is no longer because of what you said that we believe, for we have heard for ourselves, and we know that this is indeed the Savior of the world."*

10
CONTENTMENT

While being buddy sour is a very bad vice that can be downright dangerous to a rider, the horse throwing a fit because it is left behind is a big deal, too. I think horses get bored in the pasture. Out on the trail, who knew what we might see? There were so many places to go: woods, roads, hayfields past other horses, along cornfields, chasing dogs, spooking at rocks....oh, the thrill of the ride. The left-at-home horse felt pretty bad for itself and was sometimes just down-right mad. After a while, the left-at-home horse would get tired of running around screaming, especially since the ridden-away horses never answered, and it would settle down and eat until it heard hoofbeats on the road. Then the show would start again.

But one particular time, it became apparent that if a horse was left in the pasture, and the other horses were *not* ridden away, but stayed within sight, the jealousy was heightened to a fever pitch.

One fall we decided to have a "Fun on the Farm" night. We invited over a bunch of families from church. We hid clues for two simultaneous scavenger hunts, made stick horses for the kids to

CONTENTMENT

race, hid candy in a wooden box full of dried cherry pits for the little kids to find. A few of the dads brought their grills and there was about ten pounds of burgers to flip. My husband hooked up our '47 Case tractor to a little trailer filled with hay bales and gave rides to a dozen people at a time. They putted all around the farm and on some of the trails where we rode our horses. Squeals of excitement filled the air when the tractor and wagon flew down the steep hill by the garage. Janelle and I saddled up Shawnee and Merrylegs to give the kids rides, and we led the mares around the pasture next to the barn.

Before anyone arrived, we had put Dixie in the paddock with the page wire. We didn't trust her with little kids around her. She was likely to step on someone, or knock them over, or maybe even kick. She wasn't the most calm, and things could set her off. I could just see her lurching forward on the leadrope, unseating her precious burden and causing them to perform a gymnastic flip out of the saddle that wouldn't have a happy landing. She just wasn't steady. She couldn't handle it. Besides, with her safely inside the page wire, we didn't have to worry about little wanderers going under a fence to pet her, or getting zapped by the electric, since we ran hot wire around the rest of the pastures. We could turn the power off for the night and not have to worry.

Shawnee and Merrylegs were great. Shawnee even packed a kid in the saddle and the mom behind. We would lead the horses around in a big circle, lift off the little passengers, and put another kid in the saddle. The mares were docile and friendly. The kids, especially the girls of course, had so much fun just petting them and messing with their manes. I was at ease. Sharing my horses by providing something really special for these families was very satisfying.

CONTENTMENT

But Dixie was neither at ease nor satisfied. She stood at the boundary of her enclosure, head up and eyes wide. Then she would dart away, and buck her way across the pasture and back again. She tossed her head angrily. She reared up, then ran off, circling the pasture in rage. She threw herself down and rolled. All the while she screamed. She screamed while she ran and when she stood, tense and sweating, by the fence. It was quite a sideshow. Her antics gave people something to watch while they sat in their lawn chairs and ate their hamburgers and chips. People stood in groups, holding paper cups of lemonade and chatting while watching her. And she was beautiful. Jet black, gleaming with sweat, head and tail high--I'm telling you, she was a sight to see. One of the guys wanted me to let him ride that stallion. He was surprised to find out she was a mare, but I don't think he was surprised, and he may have been relieved, when I said no one was riding her.

Dixie was in good shape, and acted like that most of the night. She ran herself into a sweat, then rolled to rub herself dry, then leaped to her feet and bucked away. She was jealous of Shawnee and Merrylegs. She was furious to be left out. But her offended feelings did not teach her how to act any better around kids. Even though she thought she was being mistreated by having no attention and no job, I knew she couldn't handle the job or the attention correctly, so she stayed where she was. Maybe next time, after she was a little more trained, I would be able to use her.

Not having what we want can be frustrating and irritating. We can get to the point of throwing as much of a fit as Dixie was, only not in a horsey way. Concentrating on what we don't have can make us bitter and angry, resulting in our lashing out unjustly at others and carrying around a bad

CONTENTMENT

attitude. We get so mad at people who have what we want. We can feel cheated by God, sure he's not taking care of us properly. We can fuss and fume and try all sorts of ways to get what we want, even ways that hurt us or others.

Why do we assume not getting what we want is mistreatment? Maybe it's not good for us. Maybe it isn't the time for it yet. Maybe we can't handle it correctly. Maybe he wants us to stop fuming and look to him with faith. When God gives wealth, or opportunities, or abilities, responsibility comes with that. Our job is to be faithful with what he's given us, knowing he promised to reward that faithfulness. Contentment is a wonderful thing. It is the antidote for coveting. Contentment fosters gratitude. Or maybe gratitude fosters contentment. Knowing and believing God does what's best---because he loves us--is the key to un-coveting, which, in common English, is contentment.

A verse to hang your hat on: "And he (Jesus) said to them, 'Take care, and be on your guard against all covetousness, for one's life does not consist in the abundance of his possessions.'" – Luke 12:15

Read about it in Matthew 25:14-30.

[14] "For it will be like a man going on a journey, who called his servants and entrusted to them his property. [15] To one he gave five talents, to another two, to another one, to each according to his ability. Then he went away. [16] He who had received the five talents went at once and traded with them, and he made five talents more. [17] So also he who had the two talents made two talents more. [18] But he who had received the one talent went and dug in the ground and hid his master's money. [19] Now after a long time

CONTENTMENT

the master of those servants came and settled accounts with them. [20] And he who had received the five talents came forward, bringing five talents more, saying, 'Master, you delivered to me five talents; here I have made five talents more.' [21] His master said to him, 'Well done, good and faithful servant. You have been faithful over a little; I will set you over much. Enter into the joy of your master.' [22] And he also who had the two talents came forward, saying, 'Master, you delivered to me two talents; here I have made two talents more.' [23] His master said to him, 'Well done, good and faithful servant. You have been faithful over a little; I will set you over much. Enter into the joy of your master.' [24] He also who had received the one talent came forward, saying, 'Master, I knew you to be a hard man, reaping where you did not sow, and gathering where you scattered no seed, [25] so I was afraid, and I went and hid your talent in the ground. Here you have what is yours.' [26] But his master answered him, 'You wicked and slothful servant! You knew that I reap where I have not sown and gather where I scattered no seed? [27] Then you ought to have invested my money with the bankers, and at my coming I should have received what was my own with interest. [28] So take the talent from him and give it to him who has the ten talents.[29] For to everyone who has will more be given, and he will have an abundance. But from the one who has not, even what he has will be taken away. [30] And cast the worthless servant into the outer darkness. In that place there will be weeping and gnashing of teeth.'

11
USELESS

One thing you never know about: what will happen on a ride. And having the dog along can make things even more unpredictable. Now, Fletcher is a very good dog, and he understands the word "Out", to mean "you're not in the right place, get out", plus a few other essential commands, otherwise we wouldn't take him down the road with us. We were only a half mile from home one warm summer day, passing our neighbor's house, when I realized, too late, there were chickens in their front yard. Too late, I said, because Fletcher saw them, too. It was the first time he ever saw chickens, and I imagine they looked a lot like varmints to him.

It may have even been all right if they hadn't run. Fletcher paused to look at them, and the two red hens must have sensed his gaze upon them. My, "Fletcher, out!" command was rather idiotic since he wasn't in a place he didn't belong—yet. Suddenly, the hens darted away from the sheltering landscaping they could have crawled safely into. They opted to race across the lawn in front of the house instead. The nano-second that Fletcher paused was my opportunity to intervene and stop what was about to happen, and I knew what to do. I had to head him off. With me and my horse bearing down on him, Fletcher would change his mind in a hurry.

I pointed Skipper at the ditch and kicked her soundly to get her in front of the dog. It was only a foot and a half deep and maybe four feet across with gentle slopes, mowed short, like the rest of the lawn, and dry. She and I had navigated much deeper, weedier, steeper, and more slippery ditches than this! It was a cinch. But she wasn't having it. She danced and backed against my goading, and we lost the essential seconds we needed.

Fletcher jumped the ditch, and his huge strides quickly ate up the distance between him and the two fleeing birds. They confused him when they split up, but he quickly chose one and dove after her as she circled back.

The noise the hens made coupled with my frantic shouts at the dog soon had my neighbor and her kids out the back door of the house. One little girl ran after Fletcher, who had caught up to the red chicken and rolled it. Red under-feathers scattered everywhere and the little girl screamed. The hen, Fletcher, and the screaming girl disappeared around the side of the house. All that took about seven seconds.

I spun Skipper to the left and made for the driveway, which was the opposite way the catastrophe had gone. We clattered up to the garage and I bailed off, throwing my reins to Janelle, who was right behind me on Scout. When I reached the back of the house, Fletcher was shoulder deep in hostas, and loud squawking indicated the hiding place of his prey, not far from his nose. I grabbed his collar. The little girl ran to the hostas and brushed the huge green leaves aside until she found the thoroughly frightened hen. She lifted her out carefully and cuddled her close. Other than breathing heavily with open beak and a few missing feathers, she looked remarkably well for the wear.

I apologized profusely to my neighbor, who informed me the chickens were her kids' pets, and they thought they were going to watch Fletcher kill them right before their eyes. The little girl was crying, sobbing something about the feathers being pulled out. I tried to explain that Fletcher wasn't trying to kill the hen, he just thought it was exciting to chase it with it squawking and carrying on like that. He was always chasing the cats and mouthing them, but he never hurt them. He didn't realize feathers come out so easily. But the little girl was stricken and could not begin to process what I said.

I apologized again, profusely, and, still holding tightly to Fletcher's collar, walked, horrified, back to the horses.

"Just lead her," I growled to Janelle when she held out Skipper's reins. I was none too pleased. "She sure was useless. Wouldn't even take that little ditch when I asked her to." She and I could have stopped that whole fiasco if she had obeyed me. She had let me down. A pile of feathers hopped and flipped in the wind as a testimony of that.

Ever think of the fact that our refusal to do something God asks us to could cause a "situation"? How useful are we when something comes up and we have to decide what to do? What if the right choice looks scary or hard and we refuse to do what we know he wants? We see a person sitting all alone. We know God would want us to go sit by them, but we respond, "Nope, that's too big a leap". Someone is telling filthy jokes again. God would want us to at least walk away. But we think how everyone would sneer at us so we answer, "Nope, too big a leap". We see a need, but don't fill it. Too big a leap. Think of how our witness is lost, or how someone may be hurt, or a relationship is compromised. God's way is always the best way. Obeying, even if it seems hard, will always turn out better in the long run. For everyone.

A verse to hang your hat on: "So whoever knows the right thing to do and fails to do it, for him it is sin." – James 4:17

Read about it in Esther 4:1-17.

¹ When Mordecai learned all that had been done, Mordecai tore his clothes and put on sackcloth and ashes, and went out into the midst of the city, and he cried out with a loud and bitter cry. ² He went up to the entrance of the king's gate, for no one was allowed to enter the king's gate clothed in sackcloth. ³ And in every province, wherever the king's command and his decree reached, there was great mourning among the Jews, with fasting and weeping and lamenting, and many of them lay in sackcloth and ashes. ⁴ When Esther's young women and her eunuchs came and told her, the queen was deeply distressed. She sent garments to clothe Mordecai, so that he might take off his sackcloth, but he would not accept them. ⁵ Then Esther called for Hathach, one of the king's eunuchs, who had been appointed to attend her, and ordered him to go to Mordecai to learn what this was and why it was. ⁶ Hathach went out to Mordecai in the open square of the city in front of the king's gate, ⁷ and Mordecai told him all that had happened to him, and the exact sum of money that Haman had promised to pay into the king's treasuries for the destruction of the Jews. ⁸ Mordecai also gave him a copy of the written decree issued in Susa for their destruction, that he might show it to Esther and explain it to her and command her to go to the king to beg his favor and plead with him on behalf of her people. ⁹ And Hathach went and told Esther what Mordecai had said. ¹⁰ Then Esther spoke to Hathach and commanded him to go to Mordecai and say, ¹¹ "All the king's servants and the people of the king's provinces know that if any man or woman goes to the king inside the inner court without being called, there is but one law--to be put to death, except the one to whom the king holds out the golden scepter so that he may live. But as for me, I have not been called to come in to the king these thirty days." ¹² And they told Mordecai what Esther had said. ¹³ Then Mordecai told them to reply to Esther, "Do not think to yourself that in the king's palace you will escape any more than all the other Jews. ¹⁴ For if you keep silent at this time, relief and deliverance will rise for the Jews from another place, but you and your father's house will perish. And who knows whether you have not come to the kingdom for such a time as this?" ¹⁵ Then Esther told them to reply to Mordecai, ¹⁶ "Go, gather all the Jews to be found in Susa, and hold a fast on my behalf, and do not eat or drink for three days, night or day. I and my young women will also fast as you do. Then I will go to the king, though it is against the law, and if I perish, I perish." ¹⁷ Mordecai then went away and did everything as Esther had ordered him.

12
THE ONE THING

Rapper was a show-stopping solid black paint with four white socks and a blaze. I got him as a coming two-year-old. He was halter broke and that's about it. I spent a lot of time bringing him to the point where I felt he was ready to be broke in. I put six rides on him the fall of his two-year-old year. Once he got the hang of squeeze means go, follow the rein, and lean back means stop, he went along very nicely. Never a buck or even a balk. His three-year-old training spring and summer included not only a progression of lessons under saddle, but also leisurely trail rides out alone with just me or with my daughter and her horse. I took him over to the neighbor's house and gave the kids rides while I led him. He was a huge favorite with the kids. He was gentle and let them hug him and stroke his nose. He was the most gorgeous horse I think I've ever seen.

As sweet as Rapper was with everyone and as well as he did his job, something was horribly wrong between us.

It could be when we were walking, or if I was in the pasture working on the fence, or even if I was brushing him. If I stopped paying attention for a minute, he'd start. He'd begin by bumping my arm. Then it would turn into a nip. Normal correction, like saying "Ah!" fiercely or a jerk of the lead, didn't affect him. Once he got started, he'd sneak a nip or two more, then a bite. If I didn't have him under direct control, it was like some sort of game to him. He wouldn't back down until I came apart at him. This I know: a horse that bites is displaying a unique amount of disrespect and domination. Since I am not one to be enthusiastic about either one of those from a horse, the tension between us grew.

He was a bully in the pasture as well. He ignored the normal signs of impending trouble from Smokey, like the flick of a tail, flattened ears and tossed head, the raised back leg. He wouldn't back off until he was attacked. He would nip and bother until the gray went after him, usually ripping a piece of hide off Rapper somewhere. Rapper looked like he'd been in a war zone. His black coat was littered with scrapes and scabs in various stages of healing. I separated the two horses.

Everyone else thought he was wonderful. Oh, he knew how to act, all right. He'd stand and obviously enjoy their attention. He'd walk next to them happily. He loved the adoration and the praise. He seemed to do everything right. I could ride him anywhere on the trails. I even took him in a parade. People were stunned how, at only three years old, he would walk up to floats completely at ease with streamers and glitter and fluttering trailer skirts. He was gorgeous, well-trained, personable, and agile. He was a perfect example of how a horse should be. He knew how to behave. But our relationship stunk.

I was stumped and was nearly obsessed with research, trying training methods from renowned trainers and tips from my horsey friends. Nothing worked.

THE ONE THING

I finally realized I was getting nowhere. He needed to change his actions or change his location-- and his actions weren't changing. I sold him to a woman a few months later who was very happy with the way he acted around her. I knew it was a good match, because this woman also owned an alpha mare. That mare would soon shape up Rapper's bullying ways. Mares don't put up with shenanigans like that, and she wouldn't be as easygoing as my daughter's gelding. I also knew consequences, hurtful ones, were what he needed. Stronger, quicker consequences than I could hand him.

Consequences. Not the most pleasant word. Associated closely with 'not smart' and 'not learning' and 'stubborn' and 'strong willed' and 'bad choices'. Sometimes pain is the only way a lesson is learned. It's not the easy way. It's not the smart way. It's just the only way.

The odd thing was how he left. He loaded on the woman's trailer just fine. The trailer was a slant load, which he was not used to, but he walked right on. Then, after we loaded him in the stall nearest the door, his new owner decided to put him in the front stall instead, so we unloaded him and reloaded him. He was his unperturbed and willing and perfect self. But when I came up beside the trailer to bid him farewell, the strangest thing happened. He suddenly seemed to realize he was leaving. He scuffled his feet and rocked the trailer. With eyes strained wide, he bumped the screen with his nose so hard it came out of the opening. The new owner quickly ran up and shut the window. She picked up the screen and examined it for breakage, but it seemed fine. As she walked back toward the truck carrying the screen, I could see him inside, head up, eyes wide, ears wildly pitching, nose at the glass. He whinnied shrilly.

I stepped back. The trailer rolled away. Too bad he wasn't more worried about making sure his

THE ONE THING

time with me would guarantee his staying when he had the chance.

Life isn't about what we do. It's about who we have.

During our lives here on earth, it's our chance to guarantee our staying with God through eternity. Unlike horses, if we end up with a different owner, eternity isn't going to be so very nice. We only have one shot at it. What are we doing with it?

A verse to hang your hat on: "For we must all appear before the judgment seat of Christ, that each one may receive what is due him for the things done while in the body, whether good or bad." – 2 Corinthians 5:10

Read about it in Matt. 7:16-27.

[16] You will recognize them by their fruits. Are grapes gathered from thorn bushes, or figs from thistles? [17] So, every healthy tree bears good fruit, but the diseased tree bears bad fruit. [18] A healthy tree cannot bear bad fruit, nor can a diseased tree bear good fruit. [19] Every tree that does not bear good fruit is cut down and thrown into the fire. [20] Thus you will recognize them by their fruits. [21] "Not everyone who says to me, 'Lord, Lord,' will enter the kingdom of heaven, but the one who does the will of my Father who is in heaven. [22] On that day many will say to me, 'Lord, Lord, did we not prophesy in your name, and cast out demons in your name, and do many mighty works in your name?' [23] And then will I declare to them, 'I never knew you; depart from me, you workers of lawlessness.' [24] "Everyone then who hears these words of mine and does them will be like a wise man who built his house on the rock. [25] And the rain fell, and the floods came, and the winds blew and beat on that house, but it did not fall, because it had been

founded on the rock. ²⁶ And everyone who hears these words of mine and does not do them will be like a foolish man who built his house on the sand. ²⁷ And the rain fell, and the floods came, and the winds blew and beat against that house, and it fell, and great was the fall of it."

13
THE CURSE

When I saw Red, I knew I was going to buy him. He was standing quietly by the board fence he was tied to. But it was when his dozing head came up a little and he stared me in the eye with interest that I knew he had to come home with me. He was deep red chestnut, and, since it was December, his hair was ruffled and cowlicked, almost like a white faced Hereford. I took a look at his papers, picked up his feet, ran my fingers down his back to check for tenderness. I rode him. Then I bought him and took him home. His owners told me before we left that he had a parrot mouth. Sure enough, he looked like he had buck teeth--an over-jet in more polite company. They said it didn't affect him at all. I didn't have a clue, and I believed them. He was in good shape and not at all ribby. But a parrot mouth does affect a horse. Because horses are grazers, their teeth wear each other down and they stay lined up and short. With his upper jaw misaligned, his teeth weren't contacting correctly to wear down. I found all that out from the equine dentist. Now, I also did not know about equine dentists. But Red soon needed one.

THE CURSE

A few weeks after I got him I was concerned he wasn't finishing his hay. My other two horses ate every sliver, so I knew the hay was not the problem. Then one winter day he just stood over his hay and didn't eat any of it. I called the vet, and she gave me the number of the equine dentist when I said Red had a parrot mouth. That's when I learned that a horse's teeth just keep growing, and if unchecked, the points and barbs that never get ground off will eventually get so painful and obstructive that the horse will stop eating and die. In the wild, a horse with a parrot mouth would not live very long.

The dentist had a cancellation and came the next day. He pulled out his file-on-a-stick and did what they call "floating". The rasp of the file floats over the outsides of the teeth, smoothing off the barbs. They float the teeth in the inside, too. And they don't drug the horse, either. It really is quite terrible to watch, all that vigorous filing, the horse holding its head up high with eyes bulging, and a metal apparatus on their muzzle to keep their mouth open. I stood next to my Red horse and tried to calm him. I stroked his neck, crooned soothingly, and looked compassionately into the eye he had focused on me. At first he kept sidling over to me with little steps and leanings. I knew he was begging me to make it stop. But I didn't want to stop it. I wasn't enthusiastic about the pain, but the procedure was necessary for his very existence. The foam on his lips grew bloody because the inside of his cheeks and tongue were cut up from his efforts to chew with such sharp edges on his teeth. No wonder he wasn't eating hay!

All of a sudden, Red's big, fearful eye became hard and hooded. He pulled his body away from me. He looked forward and didn't focus his eye on me anymore. He seemed to resign himself to the pain. I could tell he felt betrayed.

THE CURSE

He was a closed book to me. He just stopped looking at me. He was obedient as ever, but the relationship was hollow. He even started acting like he was enduring his brushing instead of getting a copey look on his face like he did before. He had stopped trusting me and therefore stopped enjoying me. I wanted so badly to help him understand that his ability to wolf down every shred of hay now with no more pain was exactly *because* I cared so much for him. But he didn't connect the pain and its benefit for him.

So are we like that with God? Something bad happens and we beg him to help us, to get us out of it, to make it stop. When the thing doesn't end quickly, do we pull away, feeling betrayed? Then, after the crisis abates, do we close ourselves off to him, refusing to enjoy being with him? Do we believe God would cause or allow things in our lives that hurt us because he doesn't care?

Oh, how small we think. He cares so much about every detail of our lives. This world is a painful place to live in. The curse of sin raises all kinds of trouble and ugliness. But God is the good when all seems bad. He knows what we need, even if we can't see it, and we don't understand what's going on.

A verse to hang your hat on: "For my thoughts are not your thoughts, nor are your ways my ways, declares the LORD. For as the heavens are higher than the earth, so are my ways higher than your ways, and my thoughts than your thoughts." – Isaiah 55:8, 9

Read about it in James 1:2-8, 13-18

² Count it all joy, my brothers, when you meet trials of various kinds, ³ for you know that the testing of your faith produces steadfastness. ⁴ And let steadfastness

THE CURSE

have its full effect, that you may be perfect and complete, lacking in nothing. ⁵ If any of you lacks wisdom, let him ask God, who gives generously to all without reproach, and it will be given him. ⁶ But let him ask in faith, with no doubting, for the one who doubts is like a wave of the sea that is driven and tossed by the wind.⁷ For that person must not suppose that he will receive anything from the Lord; ⁸ he is a double-minded man, unstable in all his ways...¹² Blessed is the man who remains steadfast under trial, for when he has stood the test he will receive the crown of life, which God has promised to those who love him. ¹³ Let no one say when he is tempted, "I am being tempted by God," for God cannot be tempted with evil, and he himself tempts no one. ¹⁴ But each person is tempted when he is lured and enticed by his own desire. ¹⁵ Then desire when it has conceived gives birth to sin, and sin when it is fully grown brings forth death. ¹⁶ Do not be deceived, my beloved brothers.¹⁷ Every good gift and every perfect gift is from above, coming down from the Father of lights with whom there is no variation or shadow due to change. ¹⁸ Of his own will he brought us forth by the word of truth, that we should be a kind of firstfruits of his creatures.

14
BAD CREDIT

I don't know what spring is like in early April in your neck of the woods, but in Michigan, where I call home, one never knows. It can be very warm and spring-like, or it can be the same temperature as the inside of your refrigerator and raining.

The wind was blowing from the east when I stepped out the back door. I was glad for my winter coat and furry collar. Wind from the east is never a good thing. Ice storms always have an east wind behind them. If it's not cold enough to be ice, one can always figure on some appropriately nasty weather for the season. When I pushed up the overhead door, a blast of damp air chased shavings tendrils to the back of the barn.

"I don't know how long you'll be out," I informed Smokey as I buckled the purple and blue halter onto his eager gray head. "But I'll leave you out as long as I can."

Smokey hated the rain. One warm summer day when I didn't get him in because I figured it was a warm rain, he dug a hole almost four feet in diameter and a foot deep because he was so frustrated. I don't think he liked the feeling of the little trickles running down his legs. Or maybe it was the wet ears. But he also didn't care for being cooped up in his stall much, as was evidenced by chewed-on door trim by his stall. It was always better to let him get a little miserable outside, then bring him in. He was much more content to stand in his stall after that.

After releasing Smokey, I went back for Red. The wind whipped his dark chestnut forelock into his eyes as he head-bobbed sweetly next to me. Smokey was already getting edgy. He swooped in when Red turned from the gate, and they were both in the far corner of the pasture before I had taken a dozen steps.

The April day that started off dreary dissolved into misty rain and cold. The wind picked up as the mist became more insistent. The poor horses were soon huddled with tails to the wind and heads hanging low. Smokey stood with his front feet pulled under him and his back feet shoved so far forward there was only about two-and-a-half feet between his hooves. His head hung down much lower than Red's. He hated wet ears. It was time they come in.

Nothing pleases me more than the look on my horses' faces when they see me come to save them from such dire circumstances. On this day, however, I was being held hostage in the kitchen by my two boys, who were enjoying every last minute of their math lesson for the day--or maybe "enjoy" isn't the exact word to describe their attitude. At any rate, I called my daughter from her room where she was busy with homework, and I sent her out to get the horses. I couldn't see her progress as she ran out the back door and raced to the barn for a halter. However, I knew the second Smokey and Red saw her. Their heads came up and they stood at attention, staring toward the gate, which they couldn't see from where they stood. I knew when she

BAD CREDIT

called because they responded as one horse, gallantly braving the faces-to-the-wind gallop to the gate. I walked to the back of the house and watched as they quickly slid tail to the wind to wait for her to get there.

They vied for the halter she held out. Of course she took Smokey first, since he was her horse. Red watched for a moment, then swung his head back west, waiting for his turn with resignation. Smokey and Janelle ducked their heads and trotted the 200 feet to the barn. He turned readily into his stall. Janelle hurried back to the gate and haltered Red where he stood so he could wait another minute with his face turned from the wind and rain. The gelding then followed her out of the pasture and took the face-slapping journey happily with her to the barn, knowing his warm, clean stall and a flake of hay were waiting to help him dry off.

I watched out the window in frustration. All that gratitude and loving attention they gave her really belonged to me. I sent her. But they didn't know I was the one watching, taking pity, taking action. They gave the credit to my daughter that was due to me. I was jealous.

How many times have we said, "That was lucky" instead of saying, "That was God"? Or "That person was so nice to me" instead of saying, "God sent such a nice person to help me"? When I say "'That person was nice to me" I think I'm pretty great. When I say, "God sent such a nice person to help me", I suddenly realize how great *he* is. Giving God credit takes a different outlook. The bonus is we realize how he's always watching over us, because he loves us.

A verse to hang your hat on: "Behold, the eye of the LORD is on those who fear him, on those who hope in his steadfast love." – Psalm 33:18

BAD CREDIT

Read about it Exodus 3:1-10.

¹ Now Moses was keeping the flock of his father-in-law, Jethro, the priest of Midian, and he led his flock to the west side of the wilderness and came to Horeb, the mountain of God. ² And the angel of the LORD appeared to him in a flame of fire out of the midst of a bush. He looked, and behold, the bush was burning, yet it was not consumed. ³ And Moses said, "I will turn aside to see this great sight, why the bush is not burned." ⁴ When the LORD saw that he turned aside to see, God called to him out of the bush, "Moses, Moses!" And he said, "Here I am." ⁵ Then he said, "Do not come near; take your sandals off your feet, for the place on which you are standing is holy ground." ⁶ And he said, "I am the God of your father, the God of Abraham, the God of Isaac, and the God of Jacob." And Moses hid his face, for he was afraid to look at God. ⁷ Then the LORD said, "I have surely seen the affliction of my people who are in Egypt and have heard their cry because of their taskmasters. I know their sufferings, ⁸ and I have come down to deliver them out of the hand of the Egyptians and to bring them up out of that land to a good and broad land, a land flowing with milk and honey, to the place of the Canaanites, the Hittites, the Amorites, the Perizzites, the Hivites, and the Jebusites. ⁹ And now, behold, the cry of the people of Israel has come to me, and I have also seen the oppression with which the Egyptians oppress them. ¹⁰ Come, I will send you to Pharaoh that you may bring my people, the children of Israel, out of Egypt."

15
LAGGING

As you may well know, or can guess, bad saddle fit can get you into a heap of trouble mighty fast. The saddle I put on Regal that day didn't fit the way I liked. He was a 16-hand, long-backed appendix quarter horse, with that high wither bone I would later come to take into careful consideration when looking at a prospective horse. The gullet of this particular saddle hung precariously close to his wither when I tried it in him without a pad, but it had a soft fit at his shoulders, so I called it good enough. He didn't seem to mind the cinching when I put a pad under it, another sign the saddle fit worked for him. When I got on him, he strode right out, so Janelle and her horse, Jazz, and Regal and I headed out the driveway.

After riding a mile and a half cross-country to my friend's house, I was starting to doubt the fit. He wasn't reacting strongly, so I knew it wasn't pinching, but his stride at a walk seemed exceedingly short for such a tall horse, and his trot was teeth-jarring, like he was tense and unbending. When we arrived, my friend wanted to do some ground work with her horse before we hit the trails behind her house, so I loosened Regal's girth and let him eat while my friend and her horse worked. More friends showed up until there was a group of seven of us. What a fun way to spend a Saturday afternoon!

When everyone was ready, I re-tightened the cinch. Regal turned his head with a surprised look. I knew that look. His ears flicked back. I loosened up again and adjusted the saddle pad, which had slipped down tight on top of his wither, fingering the pad up into the gullet of the saddle. When I tightened the cinch, Regal was edgy. He shuffled and leaned. I knew what was happening. The saddle was tight. It had kind of numbed his back as we rode over, the numbness went away while the saddle was loose and he was grazing, and now that I was trying to tighten the girth, it hurt. I knew what it felt like. Most people do. When you wear a pair of new shoes for a while and take them off for a bit, then try to slip them back on, wow, all the sudden you realize how tight they were and you don't want them back on again. A three-mile trail ride ahead of us plus the mile and a half home wasn't something I wanted to do on a horse with a badly-fitting saddle. I decided to pass on the ride so I didn't sore his back. Our relationship was only a week old. The last thing I wanted to do was to make him associate pain with riding. I voiced my regrets to my riding buddies. I borrowed a halter and lead rope and turned toward home, leading Regal. My friends and my daughter rode off as a group toward the trails.

All the way home, that bay horse laid in the halter. Regal came with me, all right, but I had to have constant pressure on the lead rope. He was as begrudging as possible, making it very clear he was unhappy coming with me. He would have much preferred being with his friends, who were no doubt having loads of fun without him. He was grumpy about it and showed it with his ears hanging back.

LAGGING

My back was getting tired of that constant pressure on the lead. Nose out, head heavy, neck braced, he was not on board. Not respecting my authority, not trusting me to make good decisions, and not understanding my reasons, no way was he going to obey. He had his own interests and agenda. Plod, plod, plod. He reluctantly went along, doing just enough to scrape by. He came with me, but he wasn't *with* me.

I wonder if God ever feels like he's hauling us around while we lay our weight in the halter and plod? We don't want to follow him. Following him is boring, we think. We want to be with our friends, having fun like they do. We grump about always having to behave and be somber and prim and proper. Duty, duty, duty.

Time for a reality check! Who made us? God. Who knows how things work the best for us? God. Who understands things we don't understand? God. Who blesses when we obey? God. How important it is for us to realize we are so much better off following him, knowing the direction we go with him is the best for us!

A verse to hang your hat on: "Then those who feared the LORD spoke with one another. The LORD paid attention and heard them, and a book of remembrance was written before him of those who feared the LORD and esteemed his name." – Malachi 3:16

Read about it in John 15:1-11.

¹ "I am the true vine, and my Father is the vinedresser. ² Every branch in me that does not bear fruit he takes away, and every branch that does bear fruit he prunes, that it may bear more fruit. ³ Already you are clean because of the word that I

have spoken to you. ⁴ Abide in me, and I in you. As the branch cannot bear fruit by itself, unless it abides in the vine, neither can you, unless you abide in me. ⁵ I am the vine; you are the branches. Whoever abides in me and I in him, he it is that bears much fruit, for apart from me you can do nothing. ⁶ If anyone does not abide in me he is thrown away like a branch and withers; and the branches are gathered, thrown into the fire, and burned. ⁷ If you abide in me, and my words abide in you, ask whatever you wish, and it will be done for you. ⁸ By this my Father is glorified, that you bear much fruit and so prove to be my disciples. ⁹ As the Father has loved me, so have I loved you. Abide in my love. ¹⁰ If you keep my commandments, you will abide in my love, just as I have kept my Father's commandments and abide in his love. ¹¹ These things I have spoken to you, that my joy may be in you, and that your joy may be full.

16
FREE

I startled awake. When my bleary eyes finally focused on the clock, the red numbers were somewhere in the just-after-2:00-a.m. range. No unusual noises drifted in the open windows. A breeze was barely blowing. But I knew it was a sound that woke me up. I waited for it.

Clunk! Clunk! Clunk!! I startled again and sat up, twisting to look out the window behind the headboard. My quick movement woke my husband.

"Did you hear it?" I whispered.

Before he could ask what, the banging started again.

I jumped out of bed. "It's coming from the barn," I threw over my shoulder as I bolted out the door. Wayne was right behind me. It wasn't kicking. It wasn't pawing. It was strange. Three or four whacks in a row, then silence. We ran across the yard.

When I flicked the light on, CJ and Scout stood with great, blinking eyes, heads hanging over their stall doors. Skipper wasn't at her door. Not sure what I'd see, I ran to her stall.

There she was, standing in the corner, her left leg suspended awkwardly, buried up to the elbow in her hay net. She swung her leg, maybe in an effort to show me the problem. *Clunk! Clunk! Clunk!* The tip of her hoof rapped the stall wall as her leg rocked like a pendulum in the net. Then she just looked at me.

Horses hate having their feet stuck. Their main defense is flight, and having their feet caught is crazy-scary for them. Skipper was caught, helpless. She could have freaked out and struggled against the net, rearing and plunging in fear in an attempt to break free. If she had, she might have ended up losing her balance, and with her leg so deep in the net, she would have been suspended from it. All her weight would have been on that caught leg, and she would have done some major damage--maybe even breaking it. But there she stood, patiently rapping her foot against the wall now and again. Waiting. Knowing I'd show up sooner or later, like I always did.

"Oh, Skipper!" I admonished as I let myself in her stall. "How did you ever get your leg in there like that!"

Her leg entered the net almost perpendicular to her chest, shot through to the other side, then curled back through and ended with net wound around her fetlock and hoof. I yanked the rope end of the quick-release knot I use to tie up the hay nets for an emergency such as this. It didn't budge. Since so much of her weight was in the net because of how high her leg was, she had pulled the knot so tight on itself that the loop wouldn't undo. Wayne tried to yank it loose, but that only succeeded in shuffling Skipper back a step to avoid his arms.

I started to free her hoof, peeling the cotton cord off it. Unfortunately, with her upper leg so high in the net plus the backward step, there was too much tension on the cords. I had to urge her forward an awkward hop so I could work on freeing her knee. I bent her foot this way and that while she patiently waited for release. The final move required me to lift her leg with her knee almost to her chin. She stoically did not resist. I peeled off the last cord, and she was free. I felt for heat down her leg. She seemed to be putting weight on it fine. When I straightened, she walked to her stall door and hung her head over. She seemed to be thinking about breakfast, just like the other moochy horses in the barn.

How many times haven't we felt caught, maybe by our own stupidity? Have you ever been too embarrassed to pray because you worried God wouldn't answer your plea for help since it was your own fault you were in trouble? I sure have. Then I'd freak out and try every which way to get myself out of the predicament, which made it worse. Just as I wouldn't have thought to leave Skipper strung up in her hay net, God is so merciful, and hears us when we call, and helps us in our distress. What a great God! Yes, there may be consequences to deal with, but God doesn't abandon us. What he is looking for is our desire to never do that foolish thing again.

Perhaps while you read this story, you wondered why I didn't just cut the rope, let the net drop, and get her free quicker. Well, I had plans for that hay net. I planned on using it again. I was pretty sure once I got Skipper's weight off the net, the quick release knot would undo. Because of these other plans, what I did took longer than just a quick fix. How often we wish God would just "cut the rope" and get us out of our uncomfortable circumstances. But he has plans we don't know about, too. Sometimes help comes quick; sometimes not. The point is: he helps. He knows what's best, and that's what he always does.

FREE

A verse to hang your hat on: "Out of my distress I called on the LORD; the LORD answered me and set me free." – Psalm 118:5

Read about it in Psalm 107:1-31.

[1] Oh give thanks to the LORD, for he is good, for his steadfast love endures forever! [2] Let the redeemed of the LORD say so, whom he has redeemed from trouble [3] and gathered in from the lands, from the east and from the west, from the north and from the south. [4] Some wandered in desert wastes, finding no way to a city to dwell in; [5] hungry and thirsty, their soul fainted within them. [6] Then they cried to the LORD in their trouble, and he delivered them from their distress. [7] He led them by a straight way till they reached a city to dwell in. [8] Let them thank the LORD for his steadfast love, for his wondrous works to the children of man! [9] For he satisfies the longing soul, and the hungry soul he fills with good things. [10] Some sat in darkness and in the shadow of death, prisoners in affliction and in irons, [11] for they had rebelled against the words of God, and spurned the counsel of the Most High. [12] So he bowed their hearts down with hard labor; they fell down, with none to help. [13] Then they cried to the LORD in their trouble, and he delivered them from their distress. [14] He brought them out of darkness and the shadow of death, and burst their bonds apart. [15] Let them thank the LORD for his steadfast love, for his wondrous works to the children of man! [16] For he shatters the doors of bronze and cuts in two the bars of iron. [17] Some were fools through their sinful ways, and because of their iniquities suffered affliction; [18] they loathed any kind of food, and they drew near to the gates of death. [19] Then they cried to the LORD in their trouble, and he delivered them from their distress. [20] He sent out his word

and healed them, and delivered them from their destruction. ²¹ Let them thank the LORD for his steadfast love, for his wondrous works to the children of man! ²² And let them offer sacrifices of thanksgiving, and tell of his deeds in songs of joy! ²³ Some went down to the sea in ships, doing business on the great waters; ²⁴ they saw the deeds of the LORD, his wondrous works in the deep. ²⁵ For he commanded and raised the stormy wind, which lifted up the waves of the sea. ²⁶ They mounted up to heaven; they went down to the depths; their courage melted away in their evil plight; ²⁷ they reeled and staggered like drunken men and were at their wits' end. ²⁸ Then they cried to the LORD in their trouble, and he delivered them from their distress. ²⁹ He made the storm be still, and the waves of the sea were hushed. ³⁰ Then they were glad that the waters were quiet, and he brought them to their desired haven. ³¹ Let them thank the LORD for his steadfast love, for his wondrous works to the children of man! .

17
TOUCH IT

Prince came in thin and nervous. He was a well-bred foundation quarter horse with a thoroughbred thrown in a few generations back, giving him a lanky frame. He still had scabs under his jowl from a recent bout with strangles. I thought his shying and hyper flight response was due to some training and trust issues, and I considered myself up to the challenge. All I really did was set myself up for an education.

I read an article in a horse magazine about optical research being done on horses. I snickered about the opening paragraph talking about fitting high-profile horses with contact lenses. Intrigued by the story line, I was surprised to recognize symptoms cited for the near-sighted horse seemed to fit Prince! He was the first one in the pasture to throw up his head and stand, tense and ready to run. If the other horses even noticed anything and raised their heads to see, he was the last one to start grazing again. On a trail ride, he locked onto what he considered to be a fearful sight (usually something like a barrel or a pile of logs or a tree stump) and started jogging when that thing was far away. He would prepare to dodge or shy when he got up to it, usually darting past. This was dangerous behavior and absolutely no fun to ride nor experience on the other end of a lead rope.

Prince was cow-bred, so working cows, close up, would be a fine job for him. In a pen, focusing determinedly on the action in front of him, all decisions being fed to him from the rider to a certain extent, he would have no problem. But outside of a fence, where there were unknown variables, wide open spaces or close woods trails, where he had to assimilate details for himself and react to unknowns, he felt afraid. But, stubborn as I am, I thought I could make a trail horse out of him. I know you are probably speculating that trail riding would not be a great option for the optically challenged, but I convinced myself his fearfulness was related to environmental conditioning. Lack of exposure can easily be rectified by, well, exposure.

I took him to a trainer who taught us one of the most valuable tools anyone can have in their bag of training tricks: the words "touch it". If a horse lays its nose on something, it means they don't fear it. It was incredibly easy to teach. The trainer held a treat to the left of Prince's nose and said, "Touch it". He moved his nose to it and got the treat. She did the same to the right of his nose, then between his front legs. Then she held a brush in her hand and said, "Touch it", and when Prince stuffed his nose onto it, she fed him a treat. She had him touch a few more things, and he always got a treat. She added praise to the treat.

We went outside. As she led him past a barrel, he shied. She laid her hand on the barrel and said, "Touch it." She didn't let him move off and kept pulling his nose toward the barrel until he touched it. He got a treat and praise. We immediately moved on, which is part of the reward. He danced sideways because he still wasn't sure that barrel wasn't going to eat him. We went all around the yard. If he even looked askance at something, she had him touch it. When she ran out of treats, a proud, "There!" became a substitute. His reward became praise and being able to walk away from whatever he had to touch. Soon I could see the words "touch it" immediately made him less tense. He seemed to realize if we said it was okay to touch, it wasn't something to be feared. I took Prince home energized. How simple could something be?

It got to the point in the weeks that followed that as soon as Prince spied something to shy at and I said, "Touch it", he'd calm right down. He would walk to the thing and touch it. He began to trust my judgment on weird-looking things. He touched so many things he started to re-think the wisdom of shying at things. Did he really want to actually touch that big scary thing over there? If he let on he was scared, he knew I wasn't going to let him leave the area until he laid his nose on it.

He began to ignore things. And if he did react to something, it might be a raised head, or a stop, instead of that crazy-dangerous, cow-blocking lunge to the side. He graduated to the title of Good Trail Horse, all because of two little words.

Did you know "Fear not" and "Do not be afraid" appear 365 times in the Bible? That's one for each day! We are told many times to fear God (know what he can do and make sure we're in the right relationship with him), but as for other things, he tells us not to be afraid. Just like the two little words of assurance for Prince, "touch it", were his cue not to be afraid and to trust my judgment, the two little words for us from God are "Fear not". He's got this.

A verse to hang your hat on: "For I, the LORD your God, hold your right hand; it is I who say to you, 'Fear not, I am the one who helps you.'" – Isaiah 41:13

Read about it in Matthew 10:26-33.

²⁶ "So have no fear of them, for nothing is covered that will not be revealed, or hidden that will not be known. ²⁷ What I tell you in the dark, say in the light, and what you hear whispered, proclaim on the housetops. ²⁸ And do not fear those who kill the body but cannot kill the soul. Rather fear him who can destroy both soul and body in hell. ²⁹ Are not two sparrows sold for a penny? And not one of them will fall to the ground apart from your Father. ³⁰ But even the hairs of your head are all numbered. ³¹ Fear not, therefore; you are of more value than many sparrows. ³² So everyone who acknowledges me before men, I also will acknowledge before my Father who is in heaven, ³³ but whoever denies me before men, I also will deny before my Father who is in heaven.

18
SNEAKER

I'm not sure how it happened. I'm never exactly sure any time it happens, because it happens so fast. Or at least too fast to stop it. What I'm trying to understand is how that second horse sneaks out of the gate even if I'm leading the first one out real careful-like. It doesn't happen often. And if it does, I mean to leave an impression on the sneaky horse that makes future sneaking seem like a bad idea.

I'm sure when Bullseye snuck out that day I had a good reason for not blocking him, like I was talking to Hot Shot and wasn't paying proper attention. But good reason or not, that sneaky medicine hat gelding plunged through the narrow opening, pushing Hot Shot in his haste. The headiness of his freedom had him galloping out toward the hayfield instead of toward the barn. Which was perfect. It gave me time.

The startled Hot Shot trotted high-stepping next to me as I ran for the barn. As soon as we were in, I turned and pulled down the overhead door. And none too soon. Bullseye's hooves rang on the concrete apron on the other side of the door. Hot Shot whinnied gustily when he saw his stablemate zip past the window, but I smiled. The lesson had begun.

I led the distracted Hot Shot into his stall. He tried to follow me back out, neighing annoyingly in my ear, but I pushed him back, slid his halter off him, and latched the stall door.

Bullseye was making another pass around the barn when I stepped out the service door. With staccato whinnies, clipped short in time with his hopping, stiff-legged stop, Bullseye changed direction and veered away from me with super-fast, bolting strides that carried him quickly around the barn. The gelding had made his choice clear: he wasn't coming to me. He wanted to run. And run he would, if I had anything to say about it--which I did. My mantra is that if a horse wants to run, then I will make him run until he decides he wants to stop running and gives up. I never chase to catch. I chase to make them come.

I turned and ran across the cement apron, coiling the long lead rope all in my right hand but holding the halter loosely in my fingers. I met the runaway as he cleared the back of the barn and headed my way. When he saw me, he put on the brakes and raced back the way he'd come. I turned, too, and cleared the corner at the front of the barn as he thundered up that side. He wanted to come in, so all I had to do was run back and forth in front of the barn, while he had to traverse all the way down the side, across the back, and up the other side, where I was ready to head him off. He was puffing a whole lot more than me.

Emotions freely cross horses' faces. I'd hang 'incredulous' on the look he wore. I was everywhere! If he'd have lowered his head and slowed up, I would have slowed, too, but again he spun, and this time I let the halter fly. I had the end of the lead tight in my hand, so it fell nowhere near him, but the motion scared him. Somehow this sneaking-out thing was going south on him. I smiled.

Meanwhile, Hot Shot was in the barn, screaming for his friend. He couldn't see what was going on. He could only glimpse Bullseye flying past the windows, and hear him thundering first on one side of the barn, then the other. He could hear the choppy stops, the turns, and the fleeing hoofbeats. His worried whinnies only intensified Bullseye's plight. The runaway gelding's eyes were wide, and so were his nostrils. This running wasn't being so fun anymore.

Two more times I met him coming up the side of the barn. Each time I stepped out toward his head, using lunging technique he knew was his cue to stop. When he turned his tail to me, I let the halter fly. The third time I stepped in front of his motion, though, he hesitated. I immediately let my energy level drop, and I stopped in my tracks and leaned back into my heels. Bullseye stood, sides heaving, and stared at me. After a minute, I moved out a couple slow steps to the side, away from the barn. Bullseye mimicked my movement, keeping his head toward me. I turned my shoulder away from him and walked a couple more steps. So did he. I held out the halter. His head came down, and I crossed the distance between us. I slipped the halter on him and said some 'atta boy's. I stroked his wet neck and let him rest by me a few minutes. But instead of going into the barn, I led him back to the pasture and put him inside. I walked back to the barn and put up the overhead door. Hot Shot rumbled a greeting and strained his head over his door to see Bullseye standing at the gate. Bullseye didn't answer the colt's whinny. He was busy watching me. He dipped his head a few times in impatience as I walked back to the gate, but he stuck his nose in the halter with good manners when I held it out for him. The walk toward the barn was calm. There's so much less stress when it's done the right way: with me, with a halter on, calmly, with a good relationship between us. We had to walk around some since he was so sweaty, and I let him graze a little, but I eventually led him in his stall and gave him his grain.

Ever hear someone say they were going to "make it" to heaven? Like they had a plan, and they were sticking to it. Lots of ways to heaven, they say. After all, they were pretty good, compared to most people, and they were doing the best they could. If God didn't accept what they did, well, then he was unfair.

The way to God is not like paths to the top of a mountain, where there's any number of paths, and they all get there eventually. The way to God is one he picked, one he explained, one he made, the only one. More like a maze. And just like I was not going to let Bullseye make his own way to the barn, but demanded that he do it the right way (my way) wearing a halter and lead rope, God only allows one way (his way).

The way to God is only through Jesus. Here's what that means: we have to realize and admit we don't deserve to be near him, because he is holy and we aren't perfect, like he is. Then we need to believe Jesus was sent by God to die in our place, as a payment for our sin, since sin requires death as its penalty. Last, we need to be ready to turn our lives over to him, to follow what he says, to call him Lord and treat him that way.

It's simple to say, hard to do. But it's the only way.

A verse to hang your hat on: "[Jesus said,] "I am the way, the truth, and the life. No one comes to the Father except through me." – John 14:6

SNEAKER

Read about it in Matthew 22:1-14.

^{1} And again Jesus spoke to them in parables, saying, ^{2} "The kingdom of heaven may be compared to a king who gave a wedding feast for his son, ^{3} and sent his servants to call those who were invited to the wedding feast, but they would not come. ^{4} Again he sent other servants, saying, 'Tell those who are invited, See, I have prepared my dinner, my oxen and my fat calves have been slaughtered, and everything is ready. Come to the wedding feast.' ^{5} But they paid no attention and went off, one to his farm, another to his business, ^{6} while the rest seized his servants, treated them shamefully, and killed them. ^{7} The king was angry, and he sent his troops and destroyed those murderers and burned their city. ^{8} Then he said to his servants, 'The wedding feast is ready, but those invited were not worthy. ^{9} Go therefore to the main roads and invite to the wedding feast as many as you find.' ^{10} And those servants went out into the roads and gathered all whom they found, both bad and good. So the wedding hall was filled with guests.
^{11} "But when the king came in to look at the guests, he saw there a man who had no wedding garment. ^{12} And he said to him, 'Friend, how did you get in here without a wedding garment?' And he was speechless. ^{13} Then the king said to the attendants, 'Bind him hand and foot and cast him into the outer darkness. In that place there will be weeping and gnashing of teeth.' ^{14} For many are called, but few are chosen."

19
LABEL MAKER

Dixie was what we decided to name her. Even though she was only 14.2 hands, which is small for a Tennessee Walker, she held her unusually pretty head tall and proud, like a she thought she was a Dixie Queen. And since Tennessee is over there under the Mason-Dixon Line, it also made perfect sense. What a pretty little thing she was! Black as night, with just a star on her forehead. We met her at her barn, which was a stable dedicated to gaited show horses. Dixie had been shown a few times, but her owner said she wanted a Tennessee that was more the proper size of 16 hands, and rather disdained Dixie's diminutive stature. She was just the right size for 11-year-old Janelle, though. Since we were new to gaited horses, Janelle took a lesson from the trainer at the stable, learning to ride the way Dixie had been trained. It was odd, leaning back to go, forward to stop, foot behind the girth to turn her. Dixie was willing, even though Janelle was awkward with the new cues. Things could only get better. We loaded her up and took her home.

That October, to promote a man who was a Rodeo Cowboy Preacher and ran a rodeo Bible camp for kids, our church decided to put on a rodeo demonstration in his honor. People from our church were invited to participate in this event and viewing was free and open to the community. We had a hand in planning it, and Janelle offered to ride Dixie at the beginning, carrying Old Glory while the National Anthem was sung. Janelle's friend would be riding Merrylegs, carrying a flag with an event logo, so the girls and the horses could support each other and not be nervous. Although we hadn't taken her off our farm in the few months we'd had her, Dixie had been shown by her previous owner, after all, and we were sure she'd do fine in the big indoor arena. She did fine practicing with the flag in the pasture.

We arrived early to help set up. Janelle and her friend tacked up right away, planning to acclimate Dixie and Merrylegs to the place while it was still empty and quiet. It didn't take long to figure out why Dixie didn't work out as a show horse. Merrylegs was her usual steady self, but Dixie went into volcano mode.

Just looking at her, though she fidgeted a little, it didn't seem like there was a problem. But she was wound tight as a spring, and Janelle didn't dare lay a heel on her in case that's all it took to unwind her. Her walk was stilted and forward. If she gaited, she wanted to gallop. She ignored Merrylegs, and acted like a deer surrounded by wolves. I figured she'd calm down after a bit. I was wrong. She never settled. I ended up leading her during the National Anthem. When Dixie stepped in the arena, Janelle said, "Mooommm...", because she knew Dixie was ready to bolt or buck.

Embarrassing. But it wasn't over yet.

Part of the rodeo demo included barrel racing. We set it up so people could watch beginners through proficient racers, so those ignorant of the sport could appreciate that a good barrel racer is a highly trained, highly skilled athlete. Dixie and Merrylegs were slated to take the first two runs out of six horses. The girls had been practicing the cloverleaf pattern since we had the idea, maybe two or three afternoons. They were beginners for sure.

Janelle wisely wanted no part of it. I foolishly said I would ride Dixie. When I swung into the saddle, I couldn't believe how wound Dixie was. She was standing pretty still in the outside, but she was an equine rocket on the inside. We entered the arena and started out at a trot. She was super-sensitive to every tiny pressure of the rein, making her straight line to the barrel look like a drunken zipper. I almost forgot to move my heel back behind the girth to start her turn, which she took wide. She then spied the barrel at the top of the clover, and went for it. I reacted quickly, which, in her state of hyper-sensitivity, caused Dixie to nearly turn 180 degrees. I straightened her out. Somehow we managed to turn around barrel two without tipping it over. She charged back toward barrel one again, ignoring my earnest cuing and rein pulling. I lurched in the saddle when she suddenly caught on and veered for the top barrel. She turned it and we cantered back home, me trying to keep her in check, every stride a different length, every stride a bounce for me. At the end of our run, I sat forward and pulled her in, and she jerk-jerked, stiff-legged to a stop. After a war whoop because I did not die while riding that little black tornado, I hopped off and led her away from the other horses. To my horror, she swung around and kicked a chestnut paint horse that was walking calmly into the arena to line up for calf roping. The cowboy glared at me and told me to get my horse out of the arena.

I was coming sheepishly back into the barn after securing Dixie in a round pen, when a weather-worn cowboy rode up next to me. He stopped his calm, beefy quarter horse and leaned an elbow on the saddle horn.

"You know," he drawled, "you'd be a pretty good rider if you just got some lessons."

Now, I'm not saying I'm an expert rider, or that some lessons wouldn't do me some good. What I'm saying is, I wish I could have gotten on that half-asleep quarter horse of his and took a little spin. Or actually, that he would have taken a little spin on Dixie. You ride a wee bit different when you're strapped to a keg of dynamite, that's all I'm trying to say.

I wonder what people think of God when they watch what we do? Do they think if he was just a bit better at what he did, we wouldn't be so bad? Like if he protected a little better, or blessed a little better, or healed a little better, or controlled things a little better, we would act better and they would think more kindly toward him. Meanwhile there we are, on the ragged edge, white-knuckling a situation because we choose not to trust God in it. No one might know how hard we are for God to guide because we are too busy being overwhelmed and over-reacting and not busy enough looking to him for guidance and comfort. Dixie and I would have both had a much better time of it if she had just calmed down and looked to me for support. If we would just stop the drama, we'd make God look better, and have a better time ourselves. Our behavior makes people hang labels on God.

A verse to hang your hat on: "For you are my rock and my fortress; and for your name's sake you lead me and guide me;" – Psalm 31:3

Read about it: Philippians 4:4-9.

LABEL MAKER

[4] Rejoice in the Lord always; again I will say, Rejoice. [5] Let your reasonableness be known to everyone. The Lord is at hand; [6] do not be anxious about anything, but in everything by prayer and supplication with thanksgiving let your requests be made known to God. [7] And the peace of God, which surpasses all understanding, will guard your hearts and your minds in Christ Jesus. [8] Finally, brothers, whatever is true, whatever is honorable, whatever is just, whatever is pure, whatever is lovely, whatever is commendable, if there is any excellence, if there is anything worthy of praise, think about these things. [9] What you have learned and received and heard and seen in me--practice these things, and the God of peace will be with you.

20
RUNAWAY

That Smokey. Every once in a while he'd get a wild hair. Like that day in early March, when it was warm enough to start melting the snow away, but not warm enough to do a super good job of it. It wasn't even really snow, more like crystallized slush.

Janelle had already led Smokey in, and I was coming with Red. When we put them in at night, we always feed the horses their pellets, and they look forward to feed time, as horses are wont to do. So you really can't blame Janelle for thinking it was safe to close Smokey's stall door, but not latch it, considering she was just going to hang his halter by the feed bin and grab his feed for him. He was waiting by his feed bucket--what else would he be thinking of? Well, it was Smokey, so it's always best not to try to guess what he's thinking of.

That gray gelding shoved his way out of his stall and took off running. He careened out of the barn and headed straight for Red and me. Not one to startle easily, Red took me by surprise when he jumped to the side. In the sloping, sliding melee that followed, I lost hold of the lead rope, and the two horses took off at a gallop alongside the creek toward the road.

They took the road over the creek, and of course did not opt to take the familiar riding trail through the woods on the other side. No, Smokey decided it was a good time to explore unknown territory, at a run, and Red followed staunchly at his flank, lead rope dragging or flinging between his legs. I cringed to think what would happen if he stepped on it at that pace. Flinging clods of snow and sod, the geldings flew across our neighbor's front lawn.

Of course, we observed this all from a pitiful distance. Janelle had grabbed up Smokey's halter when he barreled out and was running behind me as we pounded after them at our dismal two-legged pace. They were out of sight when we reached the road.

We followed their tracks around the side of our neighbor's house and were dismayed and a little more than frightened by what we saw. The two horses stood, almost triumphantly, in the center of the ice on the neighbor's pond. Their muddy, snow-clod trail ended at the edge of the pond where a three-foot band of open water completely surrounded the ice that covered the rest of the pond. They had busted the fragile edge until it held their weight, so as we approached we could see their bellies and legs were soaking wet. There they stood, together, in the center of a 100-foot diameter ice field where the water underneath was at least fifteen feet deep.

We stood on the bank of the pond in angst and wonder. Just why had Smokey gone out there, and why didn't they just keep running instead of stopping where they were in most danger? Why did they just stand there facing us, almost daring us to come get them? Neither of us dared to brave the water and the thin ice at the edge.

RUNAWAY

As we contemplated how to get to them, our neighbor came up. Bless his soul, he was wearing thigh waders because he had assessed the situation from in his house and had come out prepared. He put his hand out, and Janelle gratefully laid Smokey's halter in it. He waded to the edge of the ice, broke through for a ways, and made it up on the ice. He walked right up to that crazy gray gelding and slipped his halter on. He reached over and gathered up Red's lead rope, and started back to the edge, leading both horses. We prayed their combined weight wouldn't crack the ice.

The crumbly edge proved to be a trick. The horses broke through before my neighbor did. Their fearsome plunging about had him tripping in the shallows, but he managed to keep his feet on the mucky ground somehow. All three of them were suddenly on hard ground. I think there was rejoicing all around, human and equine. Neither horse had too much pizzazz left as we profusely thanked our neighbor and walked gratefully, and calmly, home.

What a crazy escapade, running off like that, dashing around in unfamiliar territory, and then ending up in more danger than they knew! Yet how likely are we to do something equally foolish and unplanned? Folks watching us would stand stunned, shaking their heads, and say we had a wild hair. Can we expect that road to end up anyplace good, going against what we know is right, leaving behind comfort and safety and approval...and blessing? Both those horses were set up to do some blessing-receiving, but they blew it off for no reason except foolishness. Know it's wrong, do it anyway. Praise be to God that if we get off on some crazy path, he doesn't just let us go. He comes after us, ready to take us back where we belong. He leads us back. Maybe it's time for us to stop right where we are and be done with running down that crazy, dangerous path.

A verse to hang your hat on: "Just so, I tell you, there is joy before the angels of God over one sinner who repents." – Luke 15:10

Read about it: 2 Chronicles 33:1-19.

[1] *Manasseh was twelve years old when he began to reign, and he reigned fifty-five years in Jerusalem.* [2] *And he did what was evil in the sight of the LORD, according to the abominations of the nations whom the LORD drove out before the people of Israel.* [3] *For he rebuilt the high places that his father Hezekiah had broken down, and he erected altars to the Baals, and made Asherahs, and worshiped all the host of heaven and served them.* [4] *And he built altars in the house of the LORD, of which the LORD had said, "In Jerusalem shall my name be forever."* [5] *And he built altars for all the host of heaven in the two courts of the house of the LORD.* [6] *And he burned his sons as an offering in the Valley of the Son of Hinnom, and used fortune-telling and omens and sorcery, and dealt with mediums and with necromancers. He did much evil in the sight of the LORD, provoking him to anger.* [7] *And the carved image of the idol that he had made he set in the house of God, of which God said to David and to Solomon his son, "In this house, and in Jerusalem, which I have chosen out of all the tribes of Israel, I will put my name forever,* [8] *and I will no more remove the foot of Israel from the land that I appointed for your fathers, if only they will be careful to do all that I have commanded them, all the law, the statutes, and the rules given through Moses."* [9] *Manasseh led Judah and the inhabitants of Jerusalem astray, to do more evil than the nations whom the LORD destroyed before the people of*

Israel. ¹⁰ The LORD spoke to Manasseh and to his people, but they paid no attention. ¹¹ Therefore the LORD brought upon them the commanders of the army of the king of Assyria, who captured Manasseh with hooks and bound him with chains of bronze and brought him to Babylon. ¹² And when he was in distress, he entreated the favor of the LORD his God and humbled himself greatly before the God of his fathers. ¹³ He prayed to him, and God was moved by his entreaty and heard his plea and brought him again to Jerusalem into his kingdom. Then Manasseh knew that the LORD was God. ¹⁴ Afterward he built an outer wall for the city of David west of Gihon, in the valley, and for the entrance into the Fish Gate, and carried it around Ophel, and raised it to a very great height. He also put commanders of the army in all the fortified cities in Judah. ¹⁵ And he took away the foreign gods and the idol from the house of the LORD, and all the altars that he had built on the mountain of the house of the LORD and in Jerusalem, and he threw them outside of the city. ¹⁶ He also restored the altar of the LORD and offered on it sacrifices of peace offerings and of thanksgiving, and he commanded Judah to serve the LORD, the God of Israel. ¹⁷ Nevertheless, the people still sacrificed at the high places, but only to the LORD their God. ¹⁸ Now the rest of the acts of Manasseh, and his prayer to his God, and the words of the seers who spoke to him in the name of the LORD, the God of Israel, behold, they are in the Chronicles of the Kings of Israel. ¹⁹ And his prayer, and how God was moved by his entreaty, and all his sin and his faithlessness, and the sites on which he built high places and set up the Asherim and the images, before he humbled himself, behold, they are written in the Chronicles of the Seers.

21
TRANSPLANTED

Somehow, our wires got crossed the day I went to pick up CJ. When I rolled into the yard of the breeding and training facility where he was waiting for me, the owner was surprised to see me, and a little miffed at the situation. If he had planned on my arrival, he said, he would have had the weanlings up in the barn. As it was, they were in a huge pasture, at least the size of a football field. We walked over to the gate and looked at the five of them, all of which hazed away as we approached.

CJ was the tiny buckskin-colored one hanging out with a bald-face bay. The two curly-tailed colts were buddies. The three fillies were loud chestnut paints. One of them turned and looked boldly at us as we walked in the gate. The owner said she was the oldest and quietest and the one in charge, and maybe we could get a rope on her and keep the little gang close. None of them were halter broke, so the concept of getting a rope on her sounded a little sketchy to me. I had definite remembrances of how my own foal, Stormy, acted the first time I put a halter and lead on her, and she was just a few days old. These were at least five months old. But he seemed to think if we could slip a rope around her neck while we petted her, it would work. I shrugged and went with it. The filly, however, did not. When she saw the rope coming toward her, she was off like a flash, the others quickly following suit.

The owner yelled something about pinning them in the corner, which is about as easy as scooping water to a corner of a dishpan. Our quick actions only pressed fear in their little hearts and gave wings to their little hooves.

The owner said something about roping, so as he exited the pasture, I jogged after the scared weanlings at a steady, not-threatening pace to try to turn them back toward the top of the pasture. The owner's son was helping me, and we hazed the babies around the bottom of the pasture. As they started back toward the gate, they seemed to realize we weren't too awful scary, and their flight turned into a more sober, tail-lifted jog.

Three times the owner tried to rope CJ. The buckskin colt realized very quickly our efforts were being expended on his behalf, and he whinnied in fear and pressed his body close to his bald-faced buddy. I felt so sorry for him, and I was getting nervous because I knew our actions were placing a very negative wrinkle in his unhandled brain. All of us were puffing at this point. The babies broke in all directions, and the owner's son and I waved our arms and tried to cut off their escape down the pasture.

Finally, the owner sent his son for a brood mare. When the son led the mare into the pasture, all five weanlings ran to her. Even if she was mom to none of them, she was a big horse, and she was calm and safe. The son led the mare out, and the babies milled around them, bumping into each other in their quest to be closest to her. She was head-high and prancy, not understanding the anxious attitude of the frantic little ones, and not altogether enthusiastic about having babies that weren't hers touching her. She must have been a really mellow mare; she never lashed out at any of them.

In the barn, they used the stall swing doors as partitions between the weanlings and the mare to separate them from the mare and each other. CJ ended up in a stall with his bald-face buddy. Somehow, the owner wrestled a halter and lead on each of them. But the battle was still not won. We had to get CJ on my trailer. Luckily, I had an open stock trailer. I went outside to latch the big swing-door open. Half dragging and half being-dragged, the owner got CJ up to the back of the trailer. The owner got in, and the son came up toward CJ. The colt took one look at the approaching human and took a flying leap into the trailer, past the owner. While CJ cowered against the wall, the owner unclipped the lead. He quickly jumped out of the trailer and I shut the door. "There you are," he said.

After the paperwork was done, I stepped to the back of the trailer and looked in. CJ pulled himself tightly against the front wall, his big baby eyes bulging wide, his head up, his weight first on his front legs, then on his haunches. He was trapped and he knew it. Oh, dear. How would I ever teach him to trust me? And now for a trailer ride. I hoped he wouldn't have a heart attack on the way home.

After the fifteen-mile trip that I tried to take real slow and easy, I parked the trailer in my driveway. Slowly, I opened the side escape door and slid carefully into the trailer. CJ slammed himself against the back corner, his legs and body making a horrible metallic clang. My "careful" probably seemed more like "sneaking" to him. My boys, eight and ten years old, came running out to see the new baby, all excited. Nathan, who was eight, was ready to go on in the trailer, but when he opened the side door, oh, the skittering feet and banging going on! That poor colt!

I went out of the trailer and told my new plan to the boys. We got a red flat-back water bucket and spent some time filling it with long grass. We filled another bucket with water. Opening the door slowly, we eased the food and water inside. We waited a while. CJ was coming nowhere near them since they were near us, so I went inside again. Just my motion of pulling grass carefully, and what I considered smoothly, out of the bucket and slowly straightening to swing toward the weanling was enough to send him to the sidewall again. I kept my hand out but didn't advance. He finally sniffed at and whisked up my offering. I did that four or five times. He took a step up. I fed him more grass, then I backed up, hoisted myself up on the manger shelf, and sat with my feet dangling by the buckets.

Now CJ was the one moving slow and careful. I just talked encouragingly to him and waited. He snuck a few strands out of the bucket of grass, backed up, and tried again. I didn't move. When he reached over and took a drink right next to my leg, it was over. He went back to the bucket of grass and started munching. I eased off the manger shelf. He didn't shy. I started petting his back, and he still ate. It had worked! I was so elated!

I spent another hour with him, just talking and petting, letting him get used to me. Finally, I took hold of the left side of his halter, and pulled his head slow and steady to the left until he took a step. I did the same to the right. I praised and petted. Then I pulled forward on his little halter until he took a step. One more run-through of a step to each side and one forward, and I thought he was ready. I went out and got a lead rope, opened up the swing door at the rear of the trailer, and snapped a lead rope on him. I urged him forward. He took a step, then another. With that momentum, he walked off the trailer with me. I still had to lean on the rope to get a first step now and then, but he poked around the yard without spooking at things or trying to run away from me. I ran my hand down his fuzzy, wispy mane and told him how proud I was of him.

Sometimes things happen and we feel literally yanked out of one life and thrust into another. I laughingly say now that I resisted moving out here so much that the highway behind the hayfield was easy for the road crew to map--they just followed the marks my heels made when I was dragged here. It wasn't anything I was laughing at when it happened, though. Maybe you've had to take an early retirement you hadn't planned on. Or you didn't want your dad to get a job three states away and have to leave all your friends when your family moved. Or you knew things were bad lately, but you never expected divorce papers. Everything was okay when you woke up, but by the time you went to bed, everything had changed.

When things like that happen, it doesn't mean God is far away, even if it feels like it. He is close when upsetting things are happening. Have you ever thought that it is him stirring things up and moving us around? It can be pretty unnerving. But just like I meant CJ no harm and I was ready to make a new home for him, God is at work in our new circumstances. He won't abandon us or harm us. He has plans for us and things he wants us to do. Uprooted? Yes. Transplanted? Yes!

A verse to a hang your hat on: "The LORD God took the man and put him in the garden of Eden to work it and keep it." – Genesis 2:15

TRANSPLANTED

Read about it in Genesis 12:1-9.

¹ Now the LORD said to Abram, "Go from your country and your kindred and your father's house to the land that I will show you. ² And I will make of you a great nation, and I will bless you and make your name great, so that you will be a blessing.³ I will bless those who bless you, and him who dishonors you I will curse, and in you all the families of the earth shall be blessed." ⁴ So Abram went, as the LORD had told him, and Lot went with him. Abram was seventy-five years old when he departed from Haran. ⁵ And Abram took Sarai his wife, and Lot his brother's son, and all their possessions that they had gathered, and the people that they had acquired in Haran, and they set out to go to the land of Canaan. When they came to the land of Canaan, ⁶ Abram passed through the land to the place at Shechem, to the oak of Moreh. At that time the Canaanites were in the land. ⁷ Then the LORD appeared to Abram and said, "To your offspring I will give this land." So he built there an altar to the LORD, who had appeared to him. ⁸ From there he moved to the hill country on the east of Bethel and pitched his tent, with Bethel on the west and Ai on the east. And there he built an altar to the LORD and called upon the name of the LORD. ⁹ And Abram journeyed on, still going toward the Negeb.

22
CRISIS REVEALS

Every fall, the little town text to ours has a festival called the Pumpkinfest. On Saturday afternoon, there is a big community parade. Bands from the schools in the area march in it. Car clubs show off muscle cars and vintage cars in it. There are floats from area businesses and churches. Kids decorate their bicycles and ride with their friends. Veterans march in formation with flags streaming. The Boy Scouts and Girl Scouts dressed in their uniforms form platoons of marchers as well. Local farmers either drive their restored tractors through unhitched, or hitch up to a wagon loaded with bales of straw and pumpkins and farm-dressed kids. But as colorful and noisy and variant as the Pumpkinfest parade is, it wouldn't be complete without the horse brigades. There's always the 4-H group, and a cute pony or two trotting staccato in front of a cart, and a band of riders in fancy Latino dress on high-energy, high-stepping horses.

When Skipper was three years old, it was her turn to be in the parade. I'm not part of a group; usually my daughter and I would ride just the two of us, her carrying a 3-by-5-foot American flag, and me carrying a flag of equal size, white, with a big pumpkin on it. That year my daughter had to work, so it was just Skipper and me.

A couple weeks prior to the parade, I got out the Stars and Stripes and propped it, still rolled up, in the back yard. Then I fetched Skipper out and led her to it. The wind was blowing lightly, so the mellow flap, flap of the edge caught her attention. I said, "Touch it, Skips", and she dutifully walked up and put her nose on it. Then she looked away, bored. I unfurled it and walked next to her, letting the breeze blow the flag onto her back. Like a good girl, she ignored it, even when the fickle breeze turned and wrapped the flag annoyingly around her head and mine. I pawed us out of it and took her to the barn to saddle up. I hopped on and rode her to the flag where I'd propped it, and leaned down to pick it up. She touched it as I pulled it to me. When I unrolled it, she turned her lovely head and sniffed at it as it draped over her knee and mine. Then we rode around the back yard, me waving the flag, and her ignoring it. I rode her around in a big circle, the wind flapping the flag behind is, or fluttering it forward over her neck and ears. Obviously, she was okay with it. I rolled up the flag around the pole, rode Skips to the wellhead, and propped the flag against it. Then we hit the road toward some of our favorite trails.

On parade day, I sat mounted at the street side of a parking lot with about seven other riders, waiting for our respective dispersal into the parade line. We chatted and checked our watches periodically for 3:00. As the time approached, there was a stir in the band lined up on the street in front of us. Lounging kids filed into proper lines. Suddenly the drummers of the band started a vigorous rhythm. The snare drums started a staccato rap, then the bass drummers took a couple whaps at their drums. It kept going like that, *rat-a-tata-tata-tata-tata-tat, boom-boom, tat-tat, boom-boom, tat-tat, boom-boom*...The horses around Skipper and me split and rushed to the back of the lot, their startled riders taken by surprise. Luckily no one lost their seat and hit the pavement! But Skipper, after a little shifting of her feet, stood alone with me, facing the band, watching the color guard start to twirl their flags. She was so intently watching, it was like she forgot she was alone--or to be afraid.

    I was never so proud of a horse as I was of her at that moment. Unaffected by the melee of her equine companions, unafraid of something she had never seen or heard before, there she stood. I stroked her neck. She was at attention, ears pricked and head high, but she was not gathered to run nor explode. She was surprised, not scared. As the other riders eventually gathered back to the front of the lot by us, I got some very nice compliments, and no one could believe she was just three years old. What a cool horse! I was so proud of her it made me want to laugh out loud!

    Now, why did Skipper do that? Crisis simply revealed her level of trust in me. She and I had encountered a lot together by this time, and I was always doing crazy things with her. We had experienced a lot of things together. "New" didn't translate into "scary" for her. She knew I wasn't going to hurt her or let her be hurt.

    Things show up unexpectedly in our lives all the time. Some are small, like meeting new people or handling a situation at home or work. Some are big and looming, like hospital bills too much to pay, or finding out your job is being phased out. But God is neither surprised nor apprehensive, and he doesn't want us to react with fear. He knows the thing. He is always in control of it. He just needs us to expect

CRISIS REVEALS

him to do good by us. Crisis reveals our trust. Our trust reveals our faith.

A verse to hang your hat on: "for God gave us a spirit not of fear, but of power and love and self-control." – 2 Timothy 1:7

Read about it in 1 Samuel 24:1-22.

¹ When Saul returned from following the Philistines, he was told, "Behold, David is in the wilderness of Engedi." ² Then Saul took three thousand chosen men out of all Israel and went to seek David and his men in front of the Wildgoats' Rocks. ³ And he came to the sheepfolds by the way, where there was a cave, and Saul went in to relieve himself. Now David and his men were sitting in the innermost parts of the cave. ⁴ And the men of David said to him, "Here is the day of which the LORD said to you, 'Behold, I will give your enemy into your hand, and you shall do to him as it shall seem good to you.'" Then David arose and stealthily cut off a corner of Saul's robe. ⁵ And afterward David's heart struck him, because he had cut off a corner of Saul's robe. ⁶ He said to his men, "The LORD forbid that I should do this thing to my lord, the LORD's anointed, to put out my hand against him, seeing he is the LORD's anointed." ⁷ So David persuaded his men with these words and did not permit them to attack Saul. And Saul rose up and left the cave and went on his way. ⁸ Afterward David also arose and went out of the cave, and called after Saul, "My lord the king!" And when Saul looked behind him, David bowed with his face to the earth and paid homage. ⁹ And David said to Saul, "Why do you listen to the words of men who say, 'Behold, David seeks your harm'? ¹⁰ Behold, this day your eyes have seen how the LORD gave you today into my hand in the cave. And some told me to kill you, but I spared you. I said, 'I will not put out my hand against my lord, for he is the LORD's anointed.' [11] See, my father, see the corner of your robe in my hand. For by the fact that I cut off the corner of your robe and did not kill you, you may know and see that there is no wrong or treason in my hands. I have not sinned against you, though you hunt my life to take it. [12] May the LORD judge between me and you, may the LORD avenge me against you, but my hand shall not be against you. [13] As the proverb of the ancients says, 'Out of the wicked comes wickedness.' But my hand shall not be against you. [14] After whom has the king of Israel come out? After whom do you pursue? After a dead dog! After a flea! [15] May the LORD therefore be judge and give sentence between me and you, and see to it and plead my cause and deliver me from your hand." [16] As soon as David had finished speaking these words to Saul, Saul said, "Is this your voice, my son David?" And Saul lifted up his voice and wept. [17] He said to David, "You are more righteous than I, for you have repaid me good, whereas I have repaid you evil. [18] And you have declared this day how you have dealt well with me, in that you did not kill me when the LORD put me into your hands. [19] For if a man finds his enemy, will he let him go away safe? So may the LORD reward you with good for what you have done to me this day. [20] And now, behold, I know that you shall surely be king, and that the kingdom of Israel shall be established in your hand. [21] Swear to me therefore by the LORD that you will not cut off my offspring after me, and that you will not destroy my name out of my father's house." [22] And David swore this to Saul. Then Saul went home, but David and his men went up to the stronghold.

23
REALIZING IT

CJ was strange when he was young. When he came to live at my place as a weanling, we were replacing our stall walls with new tongue and groove boards. Consequently, his stall wasn't quite ready for him. He spent the build time in my two-place open stock trailer, which I figured was good practice for him. He spent the day in his pasture that had a common fence line with the other horses while they got used to each other, and when Kody and Skipper were stalled in the barn for the night, he spent it in the trailer. Hay and grain awaited him in the trailer, so at least his trailer-loading experiences were satisfying.

Perhaps it was this start that made him act so oddly. When he was pastured with the other two horses, he was stand-offish. Not really stand-offish, more like oblivious. He ate sort of near the other two in the pasture. He wouldn't eat facing them, like he was afraid of them and had to keep his eye on them. He was more likely to face the other way or be broadside to them. It was as if he wasn't part of their herd. I didn't mind this so much, as I have a great dislike for buddy-sour horses. It takes great pains to change the mind of a horse determined not to leave his fellows. The undertaking is time-consuming and can be quite dangerous. I was actually glad CJ didn't seem to mind not being near the other horses.

Later that winter, I put Kody up for sale. One day a couple came out to see him. We went in the pasture so they could meet him. Skipper and Kody walked over right away. While I answered questions, the couple got acquainted with Kody. They spent quite a bit of time petting both of my friendly horses, scratching them under their manes where I showed them the horses' itchy spots. I called to CJ. He was so cute and fuzzy. Of course this couple wanted to pet the baby. He was off in the pasture, 50 feet away, eating happily, ears up, never lifting his head or noticing we were there. He didn't come over. He missed all the scratches. Being brushed was one of his favorite things, too. For that, he would stand still, eyes half-closed in enjoyment. He just seemed to completely miss the fact that we were there. I shrugged and took Kody out. Skipper wanted to come along, but CJ didn't seem to notice we had left.

Even at night when I whistled, the other two would walk in to the gate, but CJ would still be happily eating off by himself. I could lead the other two in and he didn't seem to notice. Finally, when I'd go back to the gate, let myself in, and be walking toward him, he'd suddenly realize he was alone, and come trotting to me all startled-looking, like he had just realized he was left behind.

I had the vet out to check his eyes and ears. I started to get nervous that he couldn't see or hear right. I had never come across a horse that didn't do what the herd did. But the vet assured me his eyesight and hearing were fine. That left us making jokes about his intellect. How else could he miss the fact that we were out in the pasture? Why else would he ignore when we called? How could he miss it

REALIZING IT

when the other horses responded so happily to us? If he could see and hear the obvious, it must be he just wasn't very bright.

How often do we notice that God is there? His existence is obvious. His care is obvious. Doesn't the sun come up every day? Doesn't the rain fall and plants grow? Don't the stars grace the sky in the same formation? Yes, his handiwork is all around us. We see with eyes he designed, and we hear with ears he formed. But what about his presence in our own lives? Maybe people we know say they see him at work in their lives, but we can't see it. We call things lucky, or say "That was close!", or wonder why a certain thing happened. Are we too "blind" to see him there? Oh, that we could see him more!

A verse to hang your hat on: "Then Jacob awoke from his sleep and said, 'Surely the LORD is in this place, and I did not know it.'" – Genesis 28:16

Read about it in 2 Kings 6:8-23.

⁸ Once when the king of Syria was warring against Israel, he took counsel with his servants, saying, "At such and such a place shall be my camp." ⁹ But the man of God sent word to the king of Israel, "Beware that you do not pass this place, for the Syrians are going down there." ¹⁰ And the king of Israel sent to the place about which the man of God told him. Thus he used to warn him, so that he saved himself there more than once or twice. ¹¹ And the mind of the king of Syria was greatly troubled because of this thing, and he called his servants and said to them, "Will you not show me who of us is for the king of Israel?" ¹² And one of his servants said, "None, my lord, O king; but Elisha, the prophet who is in Israel, tells the king of Israel the words that you speak in your bedroom." ¹³ And he said, "Go and see where he is, that I may send and seize him." It was told him, "Behold, he is in Dothan." ¹⁴ So he sent there horses and chariots and a great army, and they came by night and surrounded the city. ¹⁵ When the servant of the man of God rose early in the morning and went out, behold, an army with horses and chariots was all around the city. And the servant said, "Alas, my master! What shall we do?" ¹⁶ He said, "Do not be afraid, for those who are with us are more than those who are with them." ¹⁷ Then Elisha prayed and said, "O LORD, please open his eyes that he may see." So the LORD opened the eyes of the young man, and he saw, and behold, the mountain was full of horses and chariots of fire all around Elisha.¹⁸ And when the Syrians came down against him, Elisha prayed to the LORD and said, "Please strike this people with blindness."So he struck them with blindness in accordance with the prayer of Elisha. ¹⁹ And Elisha said to them, "This is not the way, and this is not the city. Follow me, and I will bring you to the man whom you seek." And he led them to Samaria. ²⁰ As soon as they entered Samaria, Elisha said, "O LORD, open the eyes of these men, that they may see." So the LORD opened their eyes and they saw, and behold, they were in the midst of Samaria. ²¹ As soon as the king of Israel saw them, he said to Elisha, "My father, shall I strike them down? Shall I strike them down?" ²² He answered, "You shall not strike them down. Would you strike down those whom you have taken captive with your sword and with your bow? Set bread and water before them, that they may eat and drink and go to their master." ²³ So he prepared for them a great feast, and when they had eaten and drunk, he sent them away, and they went to their master. And the Syrians did not come again on raids into the land of Israel.

24
COME

It was one of those cold, windy days in the fall when gray clouds are scuttling across a heavy sky. I put Sage and Sundance out in their pastures in the morning as usual, knowing it was going to rain, but also knowing they needed a little time out for the day. Two hours later it started drizzling. I threw on my coat and trusty rubber barn boots and headed outside. I bagged a flake of grass hay in the corner of each of their stalls, then grabbed a halter and lead.

Sundance was in the pasture closest to the barn. When he saw me, he startled and ran away from the gate. The wind was at my back, and of course he turned his tail to it and didn't come when I called. I shrugged. When I got Sage in, he'd change his tune.

Sage came at a brisk walk when I headed to his gate. He got there before me and stuck his nose out for the halter. What a good boy. We jogged hurriedly to the barn and ducked out of the wind and rain thankfully. I turned Sage into his stall and let the halter drop off his head. The chestnut let out a gusty whinny.

"Thanks, Bud," I said. "That'll call him in." I bent my head into the wind and headed back to Sundance's gate. Nothing like the horse in the barn whinnying to get the one outside to their gate.

But to my surprise, Sundance was not at the gate. Not only was he not at the gate, he was trotting really fast around his pasture. I stepped inside. He took one look at me and began to run. I just stood there, halter in hand, rain dripping off my bangs and onto my cheeks. I knew better than to put on my hood. That would freak him out more. So I just stood still, waiting for him to realize I was there to bring him to his nice warm stall. Sage whinnied again. Sundance was unfazed. He kept running around his pasture, probably a hundred foot oval. When he got in the proximity of the gate where I stood quietly, he'd speed up, like he thought I was going to jump out at him. I watched him, flabbergasted.

Now, for some understanding, you need some background. I had gotten both these horses only a week or so earlier. They weren't even in the same pasture yet, because I keep new horses separate for a couple weeks with a common fence line so they get used to each other and kind of establish pecking order without being able to touch each other. So I have to admit, he didn't really know me. All he had to go on was that I fed him every day, led him quietly out to a nice grassy pasture every day, put him in his stall at night, and fed him again. I had not worked him or led him out on the trails. He came to my place distrustful, but so far, even though I didn't think I had done anything but good toward him, he had not decided to put me on his list of friends.

I watched him run around about the seventh time, still speeding up near the gate, no sign of flagging. The wind blew down the back of my coat. Rain spattered mercilessly into my hair. I was getting cold. Sage had stopped whinnying.

I stepped back out of the gate.

With one last look at that crazy horse galloping around his pasture--his fur dark with rain, his mane getting natty and stringy, his legs spattered with mud--I shook my head and ran for the barn. I pulled down the big overhead door and locked it. Immediately, it was quieter. The rain drummed on the steel siding and pattered on the door, but it was snug inside the barn. I hung up the halter and lead. I filled Sage's water bucket, and patted his barely-damp neck. He stuffed his nose happily into his hay and pulled out a nice grassy piece and chomped on it. He stood hip shot, completely relaxed. He was in a good place with good food when it was horrible out, and he was glad.

What a contrast. One horse comfortable, the other miserable. I had come for them both. I was ready to take them both. They both made choices. One decided to come. The other decided to run. The one inside called to the other, and even that didn't matter.

When circumstances around us are awful, we can respond in one of two ways. We can run to God, or we can run away. When things get bad, we can feel like God is abandoning us or feel like he wants to ruin us. We think because he didn't stop the bad, he doesn't care. We can blame him and be resentful to the point of denying his existence. Or we can turn to him and tell him our sorrows and trust him to shoulder our burdens.

God never promised to remove all trouble from this world. That's heaven. God does reach out to us in the middle of our circumstances. He promises to comfort us, to give us peace, to do for us what we can't do for ourselves, to teach us we can trust him. Staying away from him is actually opening ourselves up to more awfulness.

COME

So what is the answer when God calls? Some come. Some run. Maybe you feel like God is calling to you. Come expectantly. He promised.

A verse to hang your hat on: "Trust in him at all times, O people; pour out your heart before him; God is a refuge for us." – Psalm 62:8

Read about it in Matthew 11:28-30.

[28] (Jesus said) "...Come to me, all who labor and are heavy laden, and I will give you rest. [29] Take my yoke upon you, and learn from me, for I am gentle and lowly in heart, and you will find rest for your souls. [30] For my yoke is easy, and my burden is light."

25
NO FURTHER

There is an equestrian trail in our part of my township. It starts here in our woods that hides the creek, then meanders south, down roads, along hay fields and cornfields, through other little stretches of woods, and winds up at an equestrian trail through a township park. It's maybe five miles long or so. But there was one part of the trail we always dreaded.

My neighbor has a huge gray quarter horse gelding. You know the type: massive shoulder and wide chest, short backed and beefy, domesticated but not tame. I guess he was a pretty good saddle horse. My neighbor rode him a lot and just laughed and rolled her eyes when I called him "chesty". He was in command, no matter where he stood.

One fine riding day Janelle and I trotted out the driveway. Janelle was riding Libby, a little bay fox trotter. I was up on Prince, my dark chestnut quarter horse gelding. We turned in on the trail just up the road. It was the first time we ventured on this off-leg of the equestrian trail with these two horses. We had been avoiding it until we knew them better. Sometimes riding a trail next to pastures can be a very unpredictable thing. Pastured horses running up to the fence can be a little overwhelming, and cows...well, running cows are almost as freaky as running deer, except deer run away, and cows run up. But that's for another story.

Traversing along an overgrown hayfield while skirting a border of trees, we soon came out on lane next to a pasture of three horses. To the right of the lane was the pasture, and there was a row of poplar trees on the left. The pastured horses had heard us coming and were near the corner of the fence when we stepped onto the lane. Prince stopped in surprise, then walked on. Libby followed. The inside horses walked next to us, stretching their necks over the fence. Prince ignored them mostly. Libby jogged to show off. At the end of the fenceline, we left them standing abandoned in the corner, looking like they were pouting at being left behind. Horses are funny that way. The trail skirted the woods and started around the hayfield that would lead us right next to the chesty gray horse's pasture. Since the meeting with the pastured horses we just left went well, we had great hopes that the meeting with the chesty gray would go okay, too.

The gray and a chestnut were in the middle of their pasture grazing. We saw them before they saw us, but the gray wasn't a slacker. His head came up. We were a hundred yards away from the fenceline, but he started walking purposefully toward us at an angle across the pasture. As he grew closer, he broke into a fierce, pounding jog. His head was pulled in and his neck was bowed masterfully as he rushed to the place in the fence nearest to us. Prince never hesitated in his step. He had assessed the bully horse as he walked up, and he gracefully followed the trail as it bent alongside the pasture with hardly a look at the bodacious gray. The gray, not to be ignored, shoved his huge chest into the fence and looked beyond us at Libby.

NO FURTHER

It was while I was patting Prince's neck and telling him he was a good boy when I heard the shouts behind me. I whirled in the saddle just in time to see Janelle pulling leather and Libby's front feet come down together. The little mare tried to skitter sideways but Janelle deftly grabbed the right rein and circumvented the move. The gray gelding was chest-into-the-fence and head over, dominantly moving back and forth. Libby was just plain scared he was coming through, I think. Janelle wisely got her straight and hopped off, and stood between the frightened mare and the gray. Dragging the uncooperative bay behind her, Janelle stalked toward that gray horse and waved her arm and yelled, using tactics that would startle off a normal horse. Making your horse realize you are its protector, especially if you are in charge of the other horses in the picture, goes a long way toward building respect and trust in your horse. Unfortunately, the gray barely flinched, showing his level of respect for two-leggeds. All that melee didn't settle Libby, and Janelle had to walk her, skittering and lunging, to the end of the pasture. Those girls, neither of them, were happy.

Poor Libby didn't understand the boundary and didn't realize she was safe. Even though he was free to do what he wanted inside the pasture and becoming uninterested was not in his plan, he couldn't get to her. That chesty gray pounded next to us as we traversed the fenceline, making his presence undeniably known the whole way to the corner. But he could go just so far, and no farther.

Sometimes our situations can get pretty scary, too. Losing a job, bills piling up because of health issues, a bad relationship--worries of all kinds that are just as real as that gray horse was. But there is a boundary. Did you know? Satan wants to attack us, but God puts a boundary on him that's as real as the fence stopping that chesty gray horse. God says, "This far, and no farther" because he is in control. We are always safe with him. With him, we can face scary situations with confidence.

A verse to hang your hat on: "The LORD is on my side as my helper; I shall look in triumph on those who hate me." – Psalm 118:7

Read about it in Job 1:1-12.

¹ There was a man in the land of Uz whose name was Job, and that man was blameless and upright, one who feared God and turned away from evil. ² There were born to him seven sons and three daughters. ³ He possessed 7,000 sheep, 3,000 camels, 500 yoke of oxen, and 500 female donkeys, and very many servants, so that this man was the greatest of all the people of the east. ⁴ His sons used to go and hold a feast in the house of each one on his day, and they would send and invite their three sisters to eat and drink with them. ⁵ And when the days of the feast had run their course, Job would send and consecrate them, and he would rise early in the morning and offer burnt offerings according to the number of them all. For Job said, "It may be that my children have sinned, and cursed God in their hearts." Thus Job did continually.

⁶ Now there was a day when the sons of God came to present themselves before the LORD, and Satan also came among them. ⁷ The LORD said to Satan, "From where have you come?" Satan answered the LORD and said, "From going to and fro on the earth, and from walking up and down on it." ⁸ And the LORD said to Satan, "Have you considered my servant Job, that there is none like him on the earth, a blameless and upright man, who fears God and turns away from evil?" ⁹ Then Satan answered

NO FUTHER

the LORD and said, "Does Job fear God for no reason? ^{10} Have you not put a hedge around him and his house and all that he has, on every side? You have blessed the work of his hands, and his possessions have increased in the land. ^{11} But stretch out your hand and touch all that he has, and he will curse you to your face." ^{12} And the LORD said to Satan, "Behold, all that he has is in your hand. Only against him do not stretch out your hand." So Satan went out from the presence of the LORD.

26
WALKING WITH

I remember the first time CJ got his foot over the lead rope. We were on a walk along the road, and I spied some really nice, thick-bladed grass on the side of the ditch next to the road. I led him over to it happily, because I do love to spoil my horses. He was just as happy to bury his nose in it and rip out a huge mouthful. I stood there a while and let him eat, lead line slack between us.

That's when it happened. His left foot went over the rope as he nosed in the grass, and it slid tight up to his knee when he raised his head to chew. Wow, the reaction! He was off balance because half of him was downhill on the ditch wall, but he managed to rear and back up all at the same time. In a half a second, he was straining wide-eyed at the end rope, his left front foot held in the air between him and me. He hopped awkwardly, almost falling when his right hind foot slipped down the side of the ditch. I kept the tension, following his movement, letting him work it out. I laughed at him. I said, "You're not afraid, are you?" kind of conversational-like. He is eyes went from the rope to me, and he stopped. I bent forward and took the rope from around his leg. I stroked his leg from elbow to fetlock, and stepped back. When I just stood there, he went back to eating again.

Sure enough, he didn't keep his eye on the lead rope, and stepped over it again. When he lifted his head, it got tight again, but this time he only stopped chewing and looked at me. I leaned forward, slid the rope from around his leg, stoked his leg, and stepped back. That was the last time he ever cared a wit if anything was around his legs.

We had walked all over the place together ever since he came to our farm. Walking with me can get a bit crazy, mostly because I wore knee-high rubber boots. The boots mattered because since I had them on, we didn't have to detour around too many obstacles, water or flora. He learned to wade through slick-bottomed puddles in the spring and fall. We splashed through the creek, and sometimes headed downstream in the middle of it. I also have a habit of not staying on the beaten path. We wound our way through the woods where there weren't trails. He learned to step over logs, to duck under things when I ducked, to go through narrow places and ticklely brush, and to go the same way around trees as I did. He waited patiently while I broke branches so we could get through, and he followed me when I pulled deadfall out of the way. We watched tractors and manure spreaders go by us when we walked the roads. School buses can be somewhat unnerving when they come diesel-rattling up behind you, slow until the cab gets by, and the air brakes kick in right next to you. He got used to it. We walked next to Janelle and Scout when she rode, and sometimes friends would come over and ride Skipper, too, and he and I would walk next to them.

One wintry day the next early spring, I was headed out to take Fletcher on a Sunday afternoon stroll. When I walked along their fenceline, CJ and

Scout came over. I petted their noses over the electric fence carefully. I didn't want to drag my sleeve on the wire and get a shock, and I didn't want to give either of them a shock. I liked it when they came over to say hi. A shock on the nose when you're petting a horse can make them a bit stand-offish.

When I turned to resume walking, CJ followed a few steps. Then to my horror, he stopped and faced the fence very purposefully. Like slow motion, I saw him shift his weight onto his haunches.

"CJ! No!" I hollered. Too late. He half-reared and threw himself over the fence. Besides the foolishness of a takeoff from a standstill, he was too close in. His front legs hit the top strand, and his back legs caught the bottom wire, snapping both strands. Luckily, I have that stretchy plastic braided fencing and he didn't cut himself—but he did get quite a shock. His momentum plus the electric shock carried him down the fenceline a ways, where he turned to face me, sides heaving from excitement and a little fear. Scout ran away when CJ ripped the wire, and now he galloped back. Luckily CJ was now beyond the yawning hole of downed fence, so Scout stopped nervously near him, inside the pasture.

I couldn't believe what just happened! I was ecstatic. CJ had jumped the fence so he could walk with me! He had actually braved the electric wire in his determination to get to me!

My wonder was quickly replaced by practicality. Scout was getting worked up now because he was in and CJ was out, and the brown gelding was most likely going to see that huge hole. Even if CJ meant to walk with me, if Scout got out, he probably would start running around with his buddy. That was not a chance I wanted to take.

I shrugged out of my coat and walked up to the still-dancey CJ. When I slung it over his neck as a makeshift leading device, I hugged him. Then I held the sleeves under his neck and walked him to the barn, the still-excited Scout trotting or cantering back and forth along the fence. CJ just plodded happily along with me, ears up, ignoring his upset buddy. He didn't care where we went. I stalled him and gave him a couple of handfuls of grain. I stroked his soft neck and itched his favorite spot under his mane while he gleefully wolfed down every pellet. I couldn't help but grin when I went out to get Scout, who stood impatiently now at the gate.

Here's a thought: How eager am I to walk with God? CJ braved an electric shock. What would I knowingly suffer to be with God and walk his way? What does it mean to walk with God? When you're at a fair or a ball game, there's a zillion people you could walk with. You walk with your family or your friends--not just anyone--because you want to end up where your family and friends do. Walking with God is a journey together that ends up where he is. Walk his way.

A verse to hang your hat on: "You shall walk after the LORD your God and fear him and keep his commandments and obey his voice, and you shall serve him and hold fast to him." – Deuteronomy 13:4

Read about it in Genesis 5:21-24 (Enoch), Genesis 6:9 (Noah), and in Psalm 15.

Genesis 5:21-24
[21] When Enoch had lived 65 years, he fathered Methuselah. [22] Enoch walked with God after he fathered Methuselah 300 years and had other sons and daughters. [23] Thus all the days of Enoch were 365 years. [24] Enoch walked with God, and he was not, for God took him.

WALKING WITH

Genesis 6:9
⁹ These are the generations of Noah. Noah was a righteous man, blameless in his generation. Noah walked with God.

Psalm 15
¹ O LORD, who shall sojourn in your tent? Who shall dwell on your holy hill? ² He who walks blamelessly and does what is right and speaks truth in his heart; ³ who does not slander with his tongue and does no evil to his neighbor, nor takes up a reproach against his friend; ⁴ in whose eyes a vile person is despised, but who honors those who fear the LORD; who swears to his own hurt and does not change; ⁵ who does not put out his money at interest and does not take a bribe against the innocent. He who does these things shall never be moved.

27
LOVE IT, HATE IT

Sometimes Skipper could be a little stinker. Maybe it was just the youngster in her, but there were some days I had to revisit the question of who was in charge. On such a day, I had come into the pasture to bring water to the horses. I know it's silly, but we don't have a water tank in the pastures like most sane people. I bring water out in buckets on summer mornings so it's nice and cool. When I stall them from about noon to early evening, there's a bucket of cold water waiting in their stall. I bring full buckets to the pasture when I put them back out. I know, I spoil them, but, on the upside, no one wants to arm-wrestle me, and I never have go to the gym to body-build.

The three horses had started coming in when I snagged their water buckets from their pasture to fill at the barn, so they were waiting for me when I came back. Skipper, being in charge, claimed a bucket of her own, and Scout and CJ shared one. After just a couple of sips, Skipper laid back her ears and pushed the geldings away from their bucket. I didn't care for this horsey, but unnecessary action, so I pushed on her neck and said, "Hey!" in a sharp tone.

Skipper did not like that. She wrung her neck and trotted away, pushing the other two ahead of her. They broke apart and headed back to the buckets since they weren't done drinking. She didn't like that, either. I thought it was time to bring her 'round to my way of thinking.

I stepped menacingly toward her and shooed her off with arms in the air. She dipped her head and got a little light in the rear end. That was her mistake. I took that as the challenge it was, and a very impromptu round-penning session began.

My voice and quick, crouching movements had her and the other two horses running for the other side of the pasture in a heartbeat. They all knew the routine. They just didn't know who I was after, yet. I kept my eyes glued to Skipper. When they got to the corner, the two geldings split to the left, but I turned her right. I very purposefully followed her at a good clip, and she sped for the back of the pasture, like she was getting away from me. When she got to the fenceline, she turned left, but I headed her off and she spun to go right. Following her down the side of the pasture at a good trot, my travel took me past the confused, jigging CJ, who wasn't sure what to do since I didn't seem to be after him. I told him he was being a good boy in an encouraging tone as I trotted by, never taking my eyes off Skipper. I moved Skipper around the pasture, matching my energy to hers, never letting her stop or turn the way she wanted. I knew she would give in soon. Pretty quick now she would sling herself straight toward me and drop her head. Then it would be over.

All of a sudden, I realized both CJ and Scout were behind me, shadowing every move I made. I stoked CJ's neck once, he was so close to my shoulder. It was like they were helping me drive her. I was talking to them, telling them she was being a bad horse. I figured if I used the right tone, they could get the gist of the words. The three of us dogged her, turned her, moved her. Sure enough, Skipper quit, faced us, and dropped her head. The geldings and I walked toward her, then past her, and she joined us. I petted everyone and let myself out. The geldings were drinking water, each from a bucket, when I left.

Skipper wasn't the only one who needed a mental shift sometimes, and they all had turns watching each other being disciplined as we rode and trained them. Lots of times it was the simple, "Ah ah" they heard the trespassing horse receive. Most lessons weren't as explosive as the water bucket one. They were like kids watching each other get a lickin'. They knew when someone was being naughty.

I didn't really give it much of a thought until the day I spent on Skipper at a Judged Trail Ride. One of the trials was a 4 x 8 sheet of plywood painted white with a big, black, irregular oval painted on it. A two-foot long rubber alligator laid on the front side off to the right, and a rubber rattlesnake was coiled up at the back of the board to the left. The plywood was placed at a narrow part of the trail; there was not enough room for a horse to avoid it. To add even more flair, a six-foot tiki torch was set up at each end, and you had to pick up a wooden torch with crepe paper streamers from the near one and put it in the holder on the other side of the board once you were safely across.

When my friend and I rode up, we were fifth and sixth in line. We didn't come in too close because we could see this was a real challenge. The horse a girl was trying to get onto the plywood was refusing to put a hoof on that board. It was tossing its head and walking sideways and trying to turn around. All of the sudden, the big palomino in front of Skipper and me started popping up in front. His rider kneed him forward, but he started jigging sideways, his hooves kicking up the heavy sand on the trail.

"That's a bad horse," I murmured to Skipper as we watched him cavort the other way. My little mare stood loosely but very attentive to the struggle. I backed Skips up quite a ways to give them more room. Good thing I did. That palomino, frustrated with his rider, started backing up like a freight train. Neither one of them were looking where he was going. I quickly moved Skipper over so he wouldn't hit her. I told her again he was being a bad horse. His rider was not happy, and they had a tussle, which, I am happy to say, he lost. By this time it was their turn to navigate the plywood black hole. The palomino's rider grabbed up the wooden torch and aimed the unhappy horse at the obstacle. He stomped and tiptoed in a crouch in front of it, then half leaped and half stumbled across. In his rush, he passed the place to leave the torch, so she had to turn him back and reach *really far* to secure the torch in the holder. With it barely in place, they turned and scrambled down the trail to her waiting friends. The judge walked over to them to get their scorecard. The person helping the judge took the wooden torch and brought it to the holder on my side of the plywood.

When your horse watches all that bad behavior, they have two choices: mimic it or disdain it. When I asked Skipper to move forward, I wondered what she would decide. She stepped toward the trial willingly. She stared at the black oval while I stopped her to pull out the wooden torch from the holder, and she kept her eyes on it as we approached. She hesitated just long enough to touch the plywood with her nose, and then walked calmly across the black oval like it wasn't there, her hooves pounding loudly on the wood. She stopped politely while I placed the torch in the holder on the other side, and then walked sweetly over to the judge. I leaned down and gave the woman my scorecard. We got a nine out of ten since she touched the board before she stepped on it, but in my mind, she got a twenty. Ten for walking across and ten for making the decision to do it calmly despite what she saw the other horse doing.

When we see those around us behaving badly, we have a choice. Mimic it or disdain it. It can be easy when we see people we don't know acting out, but when it's our friends, it can get a little sticky. The question for us: whose side are we on? If we are on God's side, we will love what he loves and hate what he hates. We will watch and evaluate through his eyes. Our actions will prove where our affections lie.

A verse to hang your hat on: "A disciple is not above his teacher, but everyone when he is fully trained will be like his teacher." -- Luke 6:40

Read about it in Daniel 3.

¹ King Nebuchadnezzar made an image of gold, whose height was sixty cubits and its breadth six cubits. He set it up on the plain of Dura, in the province of Babylon.² Then King Nebuchadnezzar sent to gather the satraps, the prefects, and the governors, the counselors, the treasurers, the justices, the magistrates, and all the officials of the provinces to come to the dedication of the image that King Nebuchadnezzar had set up. ³ Then the satraps, the prefects, and the governors, the counselors, the treasurers, the justices, the magistrates, and all the officials of the provinces gathered for the dedication of the image that King Nebuchadnezzar had set up. And they stood before the image that Nebuchadnezzar had set up. ⁴ And the herald proclaimed aloud, "You are

LOVE IT, HATE IT

commanded, O peoples, nations, and languages, [5] that when you hear the sound of the horn, pipe, lyre, trigon, harp, bagpipe, and every kind of music, you are to fall down and worship the golden image that King Nebuchadnezzar has set up. [6] And whoever does not fall down and worship shall immediately be cast into a burning fiery furnace." [7] Therefore, as soon as all the peoples heard the sound of the horn, pipe, lyre, trigon, harp, bagpipe, and every kind of music, all the peoples, nations, and languages fell down and worshiped the golden image that King Nebuchadnezzar had set up. [8] Therefore at that time certain Chaldeans came forward and maliciously accused the Jews. [9] They declared to King Nebuchadnezzar, "O king, live forever! [10] You, O king, have made a decree, that every man who hears the sound of the horn, pipe, lyre, trigon, harp, bagpipe, and every kind of music, shall fall down and worship the golden image. [11] And whoever does not fall down and worship shall be cast into a burning fiery furnace. [12] There are certain Jews whom you have appointed over the affairs of the province of Babylon: Shadrach, Meshach, and Abednego. These men, O king, pay no attention to you; they do not serve your gods or worship the golden image that you have set up." [13] Then Nebuchadnezzar in furious rage commanded that Shadrach, Meshach, and Abednego be brought. So they brought these men before the king. [14] Nebuchadnezzar answered and said to them, "Is it true, O Shadrach, Meshach, and Abednego, that you do not serve my gods or worship the golden image that I have set up? [15] Now if you are ready when you hear the sound of the horn, pipe, lyre, trigon, harp, bagpipe, and every kind of music, to fall down and worship the image that I have made, well and good. But if you do not worship, you shall immediately be cast into a burning fiery furnace. And who is the god who will deliver you out of my hands?" [16] Shadrach,

Meshach, and Abednego answered and said to the king, "O Nebuchadnezzar, we have no need to answer you in this matter. [17] If this be so, our God whom we serve is able to deliver us from the burning fiery furnace, and he will deliver us out of your hand, O king. [18] But if not, be it known to you, O king, that we will not serve your gods or worship the golden image that you have set up." [19] Then Nebuchadnezzar was filled with fury, and the expression of his face was changed against Shadrach, Meshach, and Abednego. He ordered the furnace heated seven times more than it was usually heated. [20] And he ordered some of the mighty men of his army to bind Shadrach, Meshach, and Abednego, and to cast them into the burning fiery furnace. [21] Then these men were bound in their cloaks, their tunics, their hats, and their other garments, and they were thrown into the burning fiery furnace. [22] Because the king's order was urgent and the furnace overheated, the flame of the fire killed those men who took up Shadrach, Meshach, and Abednego. [23] And these three men, Shadrach, Meshach, and Abednego, fell bound into the burning fiery furnace.[24] Then King Nebuchadnezzar was astonished and rose up in haste. He declared to his counselors, "Did we not cast three men bound into the fire?" They answered and said to the king, "True, O king." [25] He answered and said, "But I see four men unbound, walking in the midst of the fire, and they are not hurt; and the appearance of the fourth is like a son of the gods." [26] Then Nebuchadnezzar came near to the door of the burning fiery furnace; he declared, "Shadrach, Meshach, and Abednego, servants of the Most High God, come out, and come here!" Then Shadrach, Meshach, and Abednego came out from the fire. [27] And the satraps, the prefects, the governors, and the king's counselors gathered together and saw that the fire had not had any power over the bodies of those men. The hair of their heads *was not singed, their cloaks were not harmed, and no smell of fire had come upon them.*[28] *Nebuchadnezzar answered and said, "Blessed be the God of Shadrach, Meshach, and Abednego, who has sent his angel and delivered his servants, who trusted in him, and set aside the king's command, and yielded up their bodies rather than serve and worship any god except their own God.* [29] *Therefore I make a decree: Any people, nation, or language that speaks anything against the God of Shadrach, Meshach, and Abednego shall be torn limb from limb, and their houses laid in ruins, for there is no other god who is able to rescue in this way."* [30] *Then the king promoted Shadrach, Meshach, and Abednego in the province of Babylon.*

28
INCONSISTENT

As very often happens, my two boys were uninterested in riding. I spent a lot of my time training, and they were bored with that. They were into jumping their BMX bikes and skateboarding. Trail riding seemed uneventful and slow to them. Maybe if I barrel raced or did eventing or worked cows... Well, the point is I realized they weren't interested in Tasha, I couldn't ride an 11-hand pony, and she deserved a new home. I put sale fliers up and listed her on the Internet.

A girl called and said she was looking for a pony for her daughter. She and her daughter and her friend came the next day. I walked them out to the pasture to meet Tasha. I like to let people see how a horse acts in the pasture. Friendliness and ease of catching is a huge selling point for me, so I figure other people appreciate knowing they won't be chasing a horse they buy from me or fighting to get a halter on.

Tasha came to the gate to meet us. The ladies and the little girl spent some time petting the little sorrel mare, who was loving every minute of it. She stood still, patient and gentle. I asked if they'd like to lead her around some. Tasha stuck her nose into the halter when I held it open for her and stood quiet while I tied it and gathered the lead rope. I handed it to the mom, and she led the pony away from us, doing some circles and leading her from both sides. Tasha followed willingly as she always did.

"Hop on her," I called. The mom stopped and looked at me kind of like I was a little crazy.

"She's not going to do anything bad," I said. "She'll be fine. Just hop on."

The mom acquiesced, and Tasha gave her a nice little walk and trot ride with just a halter and a lead rope. The mom's friend took a turn riding. They were terribly impressed.

They made another appointment for the next day to take the grandparents over to see the pony, since it was actually them who were giving the pony to the little girl.

The next day the wind was whipping and it was snowing like a mini blizzard. Since the grandpa showed up in only a sweatshirt, I haltered Tasha when we all walked out to the pasture, planning to take her to the barn. Little did I realize she planned on taking *me* there. As soon as we cleared the gate, she started speeding past me. Gone was her eager following. Now I had to quicken my step or I was going to cause a scene correcting her. I tried to put a damper on her enthusiasm, but she was intent in getting to the barn. What was with her? She hadn't led this bad since I first got her! I thought she had learned to walk with me correctly. I hoped she would stop acting like this when we got to the barn. I didn't know why she was so excited to get there. She needed to settle down!

The family followed in kind of a surprised line. I tied Tasha in the aisle and gave her a piece of a flake of hay, which she was attacking with gusto when they arrived. I gave the little girl a brush and taught her how to stroke in the direction of the hair. The mom and grandparents were eerily quiet. I didn't know what they wanted, whether to brush her, ride her, or maybe they had just come to clinch the deal. I asked if they wanted to see the little girl ride. They said to just walk Tasha around so they could see her manners.

Embarrassment and irritation grew as she alternately anticipated direction, dragged me, or lagged on her lead rope. I could not have been more annoyed. The mom came out and took the mare's lead rope as if I didn't know what I was doing, saying something about having shown horses before. Her efforts to humble that cocky pony were just as fruitless as mine. Tasha was just horrible, rebelling against every effort to control her and get her calm. I heard the mom comment about how the pony had not been like that yesterday. In a few minutes, the family got in their car and drove away.

She was like two different ponies! I was shocked at her personality switch because I expected her to be the same as yesterday. In her pasture she had acted so good! But when we headed to the barn, she was expecting her grain, or to be stalled, or something gratifying. Her behavior totally changed when she changed location. It made me look bad to that family. Sure she was good in the pasture, but obviously no good anywhere else. What was I trying to pull?

So are we always the same, consistent person, or do we change depending on our location? Do we portray a different life on Sunday than we live the rest of the week? Do we have some friends that see a different side of us than others see? Just like I wanted Tasha to be consistent, the people around us want us to be consistent, and we expect them to be. An unpredictable person is disconcerting. I was embarrassed and annoyed when Tasha changed.

INCONSISTANT

When we are inconsistent, how does that make God look to others? How does it make him feel about us?

A verse to hang your hat on: "Jesus is the same yesterday and today and forever." – Hebrews 13:8

Read about it in John 12:1-8.

1 Six days before the Passover, Jesus therefore came to Bethany, where Lazarus was, whom Jesus had raised from the dead. 2 So they gave a dinner for him there. Martha served, and Lazarus was one of those reclining with him at table. 3 Mary therefore took a pound of expensive ointment made from pure nard, and anointed the feet of Jesus and wiped his feet with her hair. The house was filled with the fragrance of the perfume. 4 But Judas Iscariot, one of his disciples (he who was about to betray him), said, 5 "Why was this ointment not sold for three hundred denarii and given to the poor?" 6 He said this, not because he cared about the poor, but because he was a thief, and having charge of the moneybag he used to help himself to what was put into it. 7 Jesus said, "Leave her alone, so that she may keep it for the day of my burial. 8 For the poor you always have with you, but you do not always have me."

29
CONNECT

Our neighbors were kind enough to agree to take care of our horses while we went on vacation. Their horses had been sold and gone for a while, but their fence was still up. As it was April, I was happy to bring my horses somewhere that had a nice shed roof the whole length of the barn just in case the weather decided to get nasty. The evening before we left, I walked Smokey there first, figuring on coming home to walk Prince and Widget over together. I should have known better than to leave Smokey alone. Before I had halters on the other two, he came home, limping badly. I ran to him, expecting to see horrendous cuts and envisioning stitches, but there were no open wounds. He just seemed unable to bear much weight on his left front foot.

I called the vet first thing the next morning. She didn't have a time open to come see him, so she prescribed horsey aspirin and set up an appointment for the next week. She didn't seem very concerned, and maybe my description of his limp didn't instill worry in her, but I was worried. Of course, after the second attempt to give Smokey 'bute, he decided he didn't like it, and no coaxing would convince him otherwise. I couldn't detect heat or swelling, and 'bute is just for pain anyway, not inflammation. He limped away the week until she could check him out. When the vet came, she was rather puzzled, which is never a good thing. She felt heat in his lower leg, but no swelling. She recommended six weeks of stall rest.

Stall rest for a three-year-old colt that is full of himself is certainly like solitary confinement in prison. Watching the other two horses eating the succulent new grass was like keen punishment, and he did not take to it. I did what I could for him by pounding in stakes and making a twelve-or-so-foot square temporary pasture with electric fence for him, moving it twice a day, so he could be contained in a stall-sized area but outside and eating. Six weeks passed very slowly. Smokey became a grumpy, frustrated horse, and I was not a fan of this personality.

When the vet returned, Smokey was limping less, but still not stepping correctly. Again, heat and swelling were not to be found. The vet decided the limp was perhaps a habit now, and even recommended leading him out or light riding.

For the next few days, Janelle walked Smokey on the lead rope to help him get stronger. He was short-stepping with his left front foot, but it wasn't horrible, and he needed exercise. Riding was fine, too, we had been told. We decided to take it easy and just ride slowly around the hayfield and maybe down a couple trails close by. Smokey seemed willing enough to follow at a slow walk behind Prince.

Everything went really well until we got to the ditch behind the hayfield. It was rather deep, but it had decently sloping sides the horses could easily navigate at a walk. Prince was walking up the far side of the ditch when I heard splashing and yelling. I spun around in time to see Janelle hit the ground and Smokey lunge away from her. He shot past Prince, but stopped when he reached the trail at the top of the ditch wall. Janelle was none too happy and none too clean. But neither of us found the situation even slightly funny. It is never a good thing for a young horse to discover a rider can be tossed. We figured the downhill terrain put stress on Smokey's weak shoulder, maybe causing him some pain, so he bucked. Janelle wasn't prepared for it since he had traversed this ditch many times before his accident with no problems. Evidently, he needed some more medical attention.

    The next step was to call a horse chiropractor. He came a week later. He slid knowledgeable hands over Smokey's shoulder and leg. He told us the colt's shoulder was rotated forward to about a one o'clock position, and his wither was pulled over. In the chiropractor's opinion, when Smokey had gone through the fence at our neighbor's, he had gotten his left front foot caught in the wire. It tripped him as it got tight, throwing him to the ground and jerking his shoulder out of alignment. The chiropractor said because the injury was at the top of the shoulder, there was no swelling or heat in the leg for the vet to find. One or two quick adjustments later Smokey's look went from grumpy to surprised to relieved. Janelle walked him around at the chiropractor's direction. His limp was almost unnoticeable. We had the chiropractor out a week later, since the limp did not disappear. He adjusted Smokey's rib cage, which was shifted over, also because of the fall. Now the limp was gone. His shoulder muscle was noticeably atrophied because of two months of babying it, but the chiropractor assured us that it would catch up to the bulk of the other shoulder as time went on and he was pastured and ridden normally again.

    Unfortunately, that smart little cow horse kept the nugget of rider-losing information in the forefront of his memory bank. Every once in a while, he'd try out the information again, and sometimes he managed to unseat Janelle. This only reaffirmed what he had already learned. Some days he was absolutely perfect. Janelle rode him bareback and double with friends. Then, every once in a while, he would get a wild hair, and off he would go into rider-testing mode. Just because he could. She never knew what kind of day it would be. One benefit of this behavior was that Janelle became much more proficient at riding a bucking horse, but that is hard to appreciate when all you want to do is just go ride and have fun. Her trust and enjoyment of him waned. He proceeded in his training and did exceptionally well as a four-year-old on equestrian team with Janelle for our local high school. In fact, he was brilliant. The three Saturdays during competition were his only exposure to showing, and he never missed a beat in English Pleasure, Western bareback riding, or speed events. He loved the showing off.

But every once in a while, even though the vet and chiropractor assured us he was completely healed from his fence accident, he would pull his bucking trick out of the bag. He had no reason to anymore, and that was frustrating. Something might set him off, or maybe he just felt moody, but whatever it was, he'd test and sometimes throw Janelle. Then he would stand there looking at her laying on the ground. When she climbed back on, it was as if it had never happened.

We can be like Smokey. Something bad happens to us, and we create a way of coping with it. Maybe the way is to yell in anger, throw a fit, or to stonewall in resentful silence. The injury of the situation is real, and we choose the way we think is best to cope. Then the situation passes, but we are stuck with a habit, a trick in our bag that we still pull out, even though our situation has changed. Our old way of coping doesn't fit with what's going on now. We know better, and we don't need to do it, we just decide to. Maybe something sets us off, or maybe we just feel snarky. It ends up creating strained relationships or hardships for us in the workplace, at school or at home. Unlike horses, we can take a look at what we are doing and evaluate how a bad way of reacting got started. Then we can choose not to react like that, with God's help, and do something else instead. Replace the bad. Substitute. That was then, this is now. Be thankful that old situation is done. And let a bad way of handling things be done, too. Handling things God's way is always best.

A verse to hang your hat on: "to put off your old self, which belongs to your former manner of life and is corrupt through deceitful desires, and to be renewed in the spirit of your minds, and to put on the new self, created after the likeness of God in true righteousness and holiness." – Ephesians 4:22-24

Read about it in Colossians 3:5-17.

5 Put to death therefore what is earthly in you: sexual immorality, impurity, passion, evil desire, and covetousness, which is idolatry. 6 On account of these the wrath of God is coming. 7 In these you too once walked, when you were living in them. 8 But now you must put them all away: anger, wrath, malice, slander, and obscene talk from your mouth. 9 Do not lie to one another, seeing that you have put off the old self with its practices 10 and have put on the new self, which is being renewed in knowledge after the image of its creator. 11 Here there is not Greek and Jew, circumcised and uncircumcised, barbarian, Scythian, slave, free; but Christ is all, and in all. ¹² Put on then, as God's chosen ones, holy and beloved, compassionate hearts, kindness, humility, meekness, and patience, ¹³ bearing with one another and, if one has a complaint against another, forgiving each other; as the Lord has forgiven you, so you also must forgive. ¹⁴ And above all these put on love, which binds everything together in perfect harmony. ¹⁵ And let the peace of Christ rule in your hearts, to which indeed you were called in one body. And be thankful. ¹⁶ Let the word of Christ dwell in you richly, teaching and admonishing one another in all wisdom, singing psalms and hymns and spiritual songs, with thankfulness in your hearts to God. ¹⁷ And whatever you do, in word or deed, do everything in the name of the Lord Jesus, giving thanks to God the Father through him.

30
NEW

We got some tack with the deal when we bought Merrylegs. We got her saddle and a few pads, a nice winter blanket, and her bridle. They were riding her with a Tom Thumb bit, which has a jointed mouthpiece like a snaffle bit, but had short shanks like a curb bit to attach the reins to. She had been previously owned by a family with kids who loved to race her, so a bit with a chin strap and shanks was a good idea for stopping purposes.
Merrylegs was a little fast, but she was a Paso Fino-cross and had lovely, smooth gaits. Janelle felt at home riding her because she gaited like Cheyenne, the beloved Old Guy, who had died from a stroke earlier that spring. Morgan was the other half of Merrylegs' lineage, and her thick, wavy black mane and tail showed it. There was not a speck of white on her trim black body.
Merrylegs turned out to be a great trail horse. She was not afraid of anything, and the other horses took their cue from her. Every once in a while, she'd do what we called a "Merry Burn". She would lower

her head when she was cantering and suddenly fly into a blinding gallop. She wouldn't turn or stop, no matter what her rider did. It was like she zoned out for a minute or three, and didn't realize you were yanking or sawing at her bit. That is a very scary thing in this Michigander-land of trees, ditches, roads, and fences. It might have been great fun out west with only sagebrush in the way. The good thing was that with her smooth gaits, you couldn't fall off. She also was not running blind, because she never ran out into the road or hit anything. She just ran incredibly fast for a ways--plenty far enough to have the rider's emotions range from dread to anger to panic--and then she'd settle back to normal.

When we got Dixie in shortly thereafter, we bought a couple of walking horse bits in honor of her Tennessee Walking Horse breed. The bits we acquired had a mouthpiece with a nice rounded tongue-relief curve in the middle, and it had long shanks that swiveled at where they attached to the bit. Dixie seemed to go really well in it. She had a nice, easy headset and didn't need much pressure on the reins to turn or stop.

One day, after seeing how well Dixie went in the bit and how fun it is to try new tack, we thought we'd try one on Merrylegs. After all, she was a gaited horse and it was a gaited horse bit. Since messing with Chicago screws on a bridle is a time-consuming business when it comes to bit-switching, Janelle just borrowed Dixie's bridle for the ride and adjusted the head stall size.

To our happy surprise, Merrylegs was much easier to control. She really seemed to like the feel of the new bit. Janelle took her for a ride that put Merrylegs through her paces and came back pretty happy. The little black horse was stopping better and turning more willingly. Because it was a curb bit instead of a jointed one, neck reining was working better. When you ride having a hand free, you're provided with all kinds of avenues for adventure and the acquisition of new skills like rope spinning or target practice. Janelle was all excited with the ride and the possibilities.

When Michelle and Laura came the next day, the girls brought in Merrylegs, Dixie, and Shawnee. Dixie got her bridle back and Janelle put Merrylegs' old bit and bridle on her when they tacked up for their ride. The three girls hopped on the three horses and headed out toward the hayfield. Usually, I wouldn't see the girls for hours. That day, they came back so soon, I knew something did not go well.

"She hates that Tom Thumb!" Janelle announced when she came in to get a walking horse bit. "I'm going to get it off her bridle right now."

"How do you know she doesn't like the bit?" I asked. "She's used to the Tom Thumb. She came with it."

Janelle laughed shortly. "It's not too hard to figure out when she's bucking when I try to stop her."

A few minutes fussing with Chicago screws and leather later, the girls left and didn't come back for the customary enjoyment-filled three hours. Merrylegs never wore that jointed bit again.

The little black horse was smart. When she got away from something that caused her pain, she didn't want to go back. She was very vehement about her choice! Once she knew there was something better, she wanted only that. I wonder if we are that smart. Sin causes only pain, yet how far away from it do we want to get ourselves? Even though we know a better way to live, we sometimes go back to behavior that only hurts others and ourselves. We go back to thinking how a person hurt us, and we ruin our day--again. We reminisce about the old days with friends and catch ourselves calling them "good", when, in fact, we know that's not what Jesus would call them. We respond with a tone we know is inappropriate, but we're so used to it that it just slips out. We have a whole new way of living when we do life God's way; the old life is done. We just need to refuse to go back.

A verse to hang your hat on: "Therefore, if anyone is in Christ, he is a new creation. The old has passed away; behold, the new has come." – 2 Corinthians 5:17

Read about it in Ephesians 4:17 through 5:6.

17 Now this I say and testify in the Lord, that you must no longer walk as the Gentiles do, in the futility of their minds. 18 They are darkened in their understanding, alienated from the life of God because of the ignorance that is in them, due to their hardness of heart. 19 They have become callous and have given themselves up to sensuality, greedy to practice every kind of impurity. 20 But that is not the way you learned Christ!--21 assuming that you have heard about him and were taught in him, as the truth is in Jesus, 22 to put off your old self, which belongs to your former manner of life and is corrupt through deceitful desires, 23 and to be renewed in the spirit of your minds, 24 and to put on the new self, created after the likeness of God in true righteousness and holiness. 25 Therefore, having put away falsehood, let each one of you speak the truth with his neighbor, for we are members one of another. 26 Be angry and do not sin; do not let the sun go down on your anger, 27 and give no opportunity to the devil. 28 Let the thief no longer steal, but rather let him labor, doing honest work with his own hands, so that he may have something to share with anyone in need. 29 Let no corrupting talk come out of your mouths, but only such as is good for building up, as fits the occasion, that it may give grace to those who hear. ³⁰ *And do not grieve the Holy Spirit of God, by whom you were sealed for the day of redemption.* ³¹ *Let all bitterness and wrath and anger and clamor and slander be put away from you, along with all malice.* ³² *Be kind to one another, tenderhearted, forgiving one another, as God in Christ forgave you.*

Chapter 5:1-6

¹ *Therefore be imitators of God, as beloved children.* ² *And walk in love, as Christ loved us and gave himself up for us, a fragrant offering and sacrifice to God.* ³ *But sexual immorality and all impurity or covetousness must not even be named among you, as is proper among saints.* ⁴ *Let there be no filthiness nor foolish talk nor crude joking, which are out of place, but instead let there be thanksgiving.* ⁵ *For you may be sure of this, that everyone who is sexually immoral or impure, or who is covetous (that is, an idolater), has no inheritance in the kingdom of Christ and God.* ⁶ *Let no one deceive you with empty words, for because of these things the wrath of God comes upon the sons of disobedience.*

31
MAKING THE TRAIL

I like a nice, wide trail. Grassy. Clean. Slow, sweeping curves. Wide, so you can ride next to your pal and have a talk. You can walk it slow, or do a little racing. There's plenty of time to figure out the line you want to take, and there's no sharp surprises or branches to duck under. You can ride kind of sloppy because not much focus is required. But I also like a narrow, twisty trail that you can't see the end of. One where your horse's head is up, their eyes are a little wide, and while they're paying attention to their feet, and you're guiding with rein and knee. One where tree branches are low, the trail is faint, and you wonder what you'll see and where you'll be when this little sidewinder trail breaks back into something more mainstream.

One fall day, I got tired of wanting to bust a trail in a copse of trees next to the creek, and decided it was time to actually do it. My two favorite tools for trail-busting are a long-handled lopper and a bow saw. We have an ancient lopper we got from my husband's grandpa that Grandpa probably inherited from his dad. Its beak is rusty, but it'll cut through a branch the size of your thumb like a hot knife through butter. Well, a warm knife, anyway. And for anything over an inch in diameter, a bow saw does the trick. I wasn't out for a wide, friendly trail. Those require chain saws and trailers to haul away the cuttings. I was going for something that took the path of least resistance.

I walked over to the other side of the creek carrying my implements of low-impact clearing ability, and headed south from a small clearing formed by a swale that allowed overflow from the neighbor's pond to escape into the creek. I hung the bow saw on a branch and cradled the lopper in my arm. Scattered in the woods were decent-sized trees, say, four inches in diameter and up, that I didn't want to cut if I didn't have to. I was mostly after the underbrush that grew in a profuse tangle among the trees. As I walked, I cut saplings out of the way and snipped low branches I had to duck under. I skirted the larger trees and cut the grabbing, viney tangles off just at ground level. I carefully chose a way that wouldn't have exposed roots or stumps a horse could stumble over. I dragged deadfall out of the way and threw fallen branches stalk-first deep to the right or left. My way through was definitely twisty. Always looking ahead, I made sure my trail didn't dead end in too many large trees too close together for passage, or up against too much deadfall for the cutting tools I had chosen. With satisfaction, I finally stepped out into the main trail as the copse of trees petered out. This was going to be a nice trail.

I went back to the beginning, by the swale, and exchanged the lopper for the bow saw. I walked the trail again, cutting back larger branches and sawing off dead trees. I cleared more deadfall. The trail was now noticeable. When I looked back, it was too twisty to see the beginning. When I looked forward, the main trail was invisible. Perfect. There were some larger branches that would have to be hauled away, but most of the stuff I cut was small and could be tossed into the woods.

When I reached the main trail, I turned and went "backwards" on my new trail, sawing off the branches I hadn't noticed when I was walking it "forward". I wanted this to be an either-way trail. I also focused on higher branches, the ones that would be winging across my face when I was astride a horse. I hung up my bow saw at the other end, and grabbed the lopper for the final run-through. While it takes a short time to describe, it took me the better part of a day to clear a single-horse-wide, winding path through that copse of trees next to the creek. I was hot and dirty and I had sawdust in my hair, but I was well-pleased when I took a last walk through that trail before heading home to make supper. With happy satisfaction I surveyed it, liking the looks of it, imagining riding my horses through it for the first time. I looked forward to it, even though I knew the horse would be walking with their head high, their eyes a little wide, and watching their feet.

. There is one thing everyone knows: if there is a trail, someone made it. Someone put a lot of preparation and consideration into the making of a good trail. Consideration of the safety of the horse and the safety of the rider. Consideration of the enjoyment the trail would bring. Consideration of which obstacles had to be removed. Consideration of the very direction of it. Think of all the places in the Bible that talk about how God makes our paths straight, sets a course before us, and leads us in certain paths. He considers us as he sets our path, and he prepares the way. Of course, some paths may make us more nervous than others. We all want to be on the wide, grassy, easy path with a friend nearby. But on some paths he has for us, we can't see the end. There are lots of twists and turns. Our confidence doesn't come because we made the path--

we didn't. It doesn't come because we chose the path--we didn't. Our confidence comes because we know who made the path and chose the path, and because he is on the trail with us. It leads somewhere...somewhere he wants us to be. The trail is always an adventure when you're out with God!

A verse to hang your hat on: "You make known to me the path of life; in your presence there is fullness of joy; at your right hand are pleasures forevermore." – Psalm 16:11

Read about it in Proverbs 2:1-15.

¹ My son, if you receive my words and treasure up my commandments with you, ² making your ear attentive to wisdom and inclining your heart to understanding; ³ yes, if you call out for insight and raise your voice for understanding, ⁴ if you seek it like silver and search for it as for hidden treasures, ⁵ then you will understand the fear of the LORD and find the knowledge of God. ⁶ For the LORD gives wisdom; from his mouth come knowledge and understanding; ⁷ he stores up sound wisdom for the upright; he is a shield to those who walk in integrity, ⁸ guarding the paths of justice and watching over the way of his saints. ⁹ Then you will understand righteousness and justice and equity, every good path; ¹⁰ for wisdom will come into your heart, and knowledge will be pleasant to your soul; ¹¹ discretion will watch over you, understanding will guard you, ¹² delivering you from the way of evil, from men of perverted speech, ¹³ who forsake the paths of uprightness to walk in the ways of darkness, ¹⁴ who rejoice in doing evil and delight in the perverseness of evil, ¹⁵ men whose paths are crooked, and who are devious in their ways.

ABOUT THE AUTHOR

Connie Van Huis has been infected with what she calls "horse fever" since she was young. She grew up reading books about horses and wanted nothing more than a horse of her own. Luckily, her neighbors had ponies and were only too happy to have her ride them. Still, she couldn't wait for the day when she finally could call a horse her own. When she was fourteen, she bought a five-month-old weanling, and her journey toward learning to train horses had its modest beginning. Years later, she and her daughter began buying horses to ride and train and resell. When Connie realized how often she was using stories of what happened between her and her horses as illustrations when she was teaching Sunday school and talking with friends, she began writing the lessons down.

Connie and her husband and three children live in Michigan. Her favorite type of riding is exploring trails, challenging her horse to trust and obey, ready to be proud of her willing partner. Going off road in Jeeps is something the whole family does together.

Other books coming soon by this author:

More Stable Help (volume 2 to this devotional)

Sunday school/Bible study material:
Meeting God in the Wilderness: Sunday School Lessons, 4th Grade and Up
The Rose on the Thorns: Learning to Be An Esther
Vintage Christmas Programs for Children

Western Fiction:
Between Here and There: The Journey of Cammy Densmore

Made in the USA
Columbia, SC
05 December 2017